As the pastor of a church that draws many spiritual seekers and new believers, I am always chagrined when a book like Bart Ehrman's *Misquoting Jesus* becomes a best seller. Perrin sets the record straight and lays a solid foundation for faith in the Jesus of Scripture. I'll be buying extra copies of *Lost in Transmission?* for my friends.

— JIM NICODEM
is Senior Pastor at Christ Community
Church, St. Charles, IL, a Willow Creek
Associate church

With an engaging narrative and autobiographical style, Nick Perrin gently refutes the claims of Bart Ehrman and others who challenge the reliability of the New Testament gospels. While one might expect an agnostic historian like Ehrman to be a more objective critic of the Jesus tradition, it is Perrin instead who comes across balanced and even-handed, acknowledging problems honestly but providing a reasonable assessment of the philosophical and historical foundations of the quest for the real Jesus. Anyone reading this volume beside Ehrman's *Misquoting Jesus* or *Lost Christianities* should quickly recognize which author is prone to exaggeration and generalization and which is not. This is a great book for anyone with honest doubts or questions concerning the evidence for the historical Jesus.

— MARK STRAUSS,
Professor of New Testament at Bethel
Seminary in San Diego and author of
Four Portraits, One Jesus

This is an outstanding book. It is a beautifully written combination of personal stories from Nick Perrin's own life, a careful and respectful presentation of critical views of Jesus and the New Testament—especially those of Bart Ehrman, a powerful and compelling refutation of those views, and a clear and joyful celebration of the trustworthiness of the biblical text and the gospel of Christ. There is no doubt in my mind that this is one of the finest defenses of true biblical Christianity to be published in many years. I know of only a few books that communicate our Christian faith in a way that will be immediately accessible to non-Christians; this is certainly one of them. I know several unbelieving friends, as well as many struggling Christian believers, to whom I want to give this book as soon as possible. Read it; reread it; buy more copies; give them away.

— JERRAM BARRS,
Professor of Christianity and
Contemporary Culture, and Resident
Scholar of the Francis Schaeffer Institute,
Covenant Theological Seminary,
St. Louis, Missouri.

In this volume Nick Perrin provides an intelligent, engaging, and vigorous response to recent and longstanding claims that the teachings of Jesus have been lost in ancient history. All those interested in the substance of these increasingly common assertions will profit from this book and may also gain a better understanding concerning the nature of the Bible.

— JOHN R. FRANKE,
Professor of Theology at Biblical
Seminary

OTHER BOOKS BY NICHOLAS PERRIN

Thomas, the Other Gospel

The Judas Gospel

Questioning Q: A Multidimensional Critique
(with Mark S. Goodacre)

Thomas and Tatian

LOST IN TRANS MISSION?

WHAT WE CAN KNOW ABOUT
THE WORDS OF JESUS

BY NICHOLAS PERRIN

THOMAS NELSON
Since 1798

NASHVILLE   DALLAS   MEXICO CITY   RIO DE JANEIRO   BEIJING

Published in Nashville, Tennessee, by Thomas Nelson. Thomas Nelson is a registered trademark of Thomas Nelson, Inc.

Thomas Nelson, Inc. titles may be purchased in bulk for educational, business, fund-raising, or sales promotional use. For information, please e-mail SpecialMarkets@ThomasNelson.com.

All Scripture quotations, unless otherwise indicated, are taken from the New King James Version (NKJV), © 1979, 1980, 1982, Thomas Nelson, Inc., Publishers.

Editorial Staff: Greg Daniel, acquisition editor, and Thom Chittom, managing editor
Cover Design: Micah Kandras
Page Design: Walter Petrie

Library of Congress Cataloging-in-Publication Data

Perrin, Nicholas.
    Lost in transmission? : what we can and cannot know about the words of Jesus / by Nicholas Perrin.
        p. cm.
    Includes bibliographical references and index.
    ISBN: -0-8499-2942-3
    1. Jesus Christ—Historicity. 2. Bible—Evidences, authority, etc. I. Title.
BT303.2.P44 2007
232.9'08—dc22   2007023782

Printed in the United States of America

07 08 09 10 11 QW 5 4 3 2 1

For my father and mother

CONTENTS

FOREWORD

When Greg Daniel at Thomas Nelson Inc. first brought up the prospect of my writing a book responding to Bart Ehrman's runaway best seller, *Misquoting Jesus*, I confess I was slightly skeptical. Feeling snowed under by various writing projects and thinking it would be more appropriate to have a text-critical specialist (that is, a New Testament scholar whose primary research interest is in the transmission of New Testament manuscripts) respond to a book about text criticism, I was initially of the mind to decline. But the more I thought about it, and the more I thought about what Ehrman was really doing in his book, the more I thought, *Maybe something* else *needs to be said about all this after all.*

While are a handful of books on the market have sought to respond to Bart Ehrman by sparring with the particulars of his thesis on a scholarly yet popular level, this book is less about engaging Ehrman's points directly (although there is some of that here) and more about engaging them indirectly. I approach the matter this way because while I am interested in what Ehrman (not to mention many other New Testament scholars) believes about what we can know about the words of Jesus, I am just as interested in *how* he believes. Here, I am not so interested in arguing with him point by point (although again there is some of that here) but in allowing him to make me think through my own position. What *can* we really know about the words of Jesus?

More often than we care to admit, intellectual journeys run parallel to spiritual journeys. Our dispositions, our sense of what is good and beautiful, and our spiritual journeys cannot be separated from our sifting and interpreting of the historical data. That is why I want to tell my story. If Bart Ehrman, having been confronted with an alleged problem in the gospel of Mark, decided to put away the evangelicalism of his youth for a purportedly more mature agnostic position, then my story, also involving the gospel of Mark, runs in the opposite direction. But my goal here is not to chide Ehrman, or anyone else for that matter, for his spiritual stance, nor is my major beef with Ehrman's history (although I disagree at a number of points). Instead and above all, I am interested in getting readers of this book to think about how we know about Jesus and his words.

This book is for different kinds of people. It is for the countless people out there who, though interested in Jesus, are *afraid to believe* because they think that we cannot know anything about him or his words. It is also for Christians who are *afraid to think* because they believe we cannot know anything about Jesus. And it is for Christians who, being *unafraid to believe or think*, have dared to ascend the intellectual climbing wall of their faith, but who, having been harnessed into the Enlightenment understanding of historical evidence, are unaware of the fragility of that harness.

If Ehrman converted from unbelief to belief and back again, his spiritual-intellectual autobiography shows no signs of his ever having budged in his epistemology, in the way he answers the question "How can we know anything at all from history?" Christians have long talked about converting souls; it's time they talk more about converting the faculty of reason and reorienting the whole "how we can know" question. This book is about my journey on which I finally settled that question in my own mind.

IMAGINE

I first "met" the Bible in the spring of 1981, when I was a high school junior at Phillips Exeter Academy, a New England boarding school. I had been taking Latin for four years, and while I was washing out in nearly every subject, the language of the Romans was one of the few things I could manage. Having been encouraged to take Greek my senior year, I decided to buy and study the assigned Greek grammar ahead of time. Before I knew it, I had taught myself to read the funny squiggles and was eager to try out my translation skills on real texts, not just the ancient Greek equivalent of "See Spot run."

Soon enough, while browsing through some discontinued books for sale in the school library, I saw my chance. It was a copy of Westcott and Hort's *The New Testament in the Original Greek*, on sale for something like a dollar. I bought it, took it home, and started reading the gospel of Mark in its original language. That was the first time, as far as I know, that I had read the Bible.

Although I have a dim memory of attending an occasional flannelgraph-style Sunday school as a very small child, I did not grow up in the church. I was not part of a churchgoing family. The only Christians I knew were people who, quite frankly, never demonstrably applied their faith to the way they went about life. So in opening up the gospel of Mark, I had no guides to fall back on; I had no idea what I was doing. Nor did I have any idea what I would find.

I read through the first chapters slowly and carefully (you can't help reading slowly when you're looking up every other word), and I was beginning to make some sense of what the text was saying about Jesus. *Pretty cool stuff,* I thought to myself. *Is it possible that God could exist after all?* It was still too early in my journey for me to discern what exactly the New Testament writings were really asking of me, although I realized even then that they in fact seemed to be demanding *something* of me—a response of some kind. At the time, I just wasn't sure what it was.

Meanwhile, I continued, as I had spare moments, to plod through the Greek. I also continued to read anything else that might help me refute, corroborate, or otherwise process what was to become my favorite gospel, Mark. (For some reason, I was always looking for almost any excuse to read something other than the books that I was supposed to read for my classes.) I remember how after a frigid bus trip down to Cambridge, my friends and I went inside the Harvard Co-op Bookstore to warm up. I ended up buying Friedrich Nietzsche's *Thus Spoke Zarathrustra* and Sugerman and Hopkins's *No One Here Gets Out Alive,* a biography about Jim Morrison, the lead singer for the Doors, my favorite group at the time. Hours later back in my warm dormitory room, I dived right into both books. Nietzsche and Morrison both seemed, in their own ways, to take Christianity seriously, even if their postures were intensely oppositional. *Maybe,* I thought, *I will come to think like them.*

During those days the radio airwaves were rife with Beatles music, largely in tribute to John Lennon, who had been gunned down only a few months before. Although Lennon's most famous song, "Imagine," had been out for years, the song was revived as if it were new and fresh. Its message was an invitation to imagine the peaceful bliss of a world without heaven or religion.

Having grown up and experienced life in a world that didn't concern itself much with "religion," I felt the song resonated with me. No heaven? Imagine that. If we could just get people to forget about heaven, then we would all be better off, redirecting our energies in a much more useful way. If we would cut out all this talk of religion and eternal destinies, Hindus could stop being Hindus, Muslims could stop being Muslims, Christians could stop being Christians, and Jews could stop being Jews. They could all lay aside their destructive religious differences, and finally we could all pull together and get along. It made perfect sense. What a novel idea— what an ingenious song.

Looking back today, I realize that the message of "Imagine" is neither particularly novel nor ingenious. At least in the West, people have been saying pretty much the same thing since the time of the French Enlightenment thinker Jean-Jacques Rousseau (1712–78). While I have been a Beatles fan since first grade and would be the last to doubt John Lennon's genius as a songwriter, the words of this song (the lyrics of which actually now purport to come from his then wife, Yoko Ono) hardly demand creative genius. It takes no William Wordsworth, at any rate, to say exactly what Western culture has been saying for the past quarter of a millennium and in much the same way. In the end, John Lennon is saying, "I wish everybody looked at life the way I did—I and the rest of the Enlightenment." Of course, that's the poet's prerogative.

But if you get what "Imagine" is driving at, as well as our own cultural location, you're pretty well positioned for understanding the song's popularity too. And popular it has been. One would be hard-pressed to think of more than five songs in rock 'n' roll history more admired than this song. According to the 2002 *Guinness World Records: British Hit Singles*, "Imagine" was the second most popular song in Britain (second only to Queen's "Bohemian Rhapsody"). When the far-reaching Musicradio WABC-AM signed off the air in the spring of 1982, Lennon's song was chosen to be the final song; "Imagine" gave voice to the last words of a cultural institution, the swan song of an era. It has been replayed, resung, and remixed countless times to the delight of equally countless audiences. Presumably these same audiences have found, as I did some years ago, that there is something alluring about the idea of a heavenless, religionless "brotherhood of man." But even if the substance of this vision, which again traces its origins right back to the salons of eighteenth-century French *philosophes*, were today to strike me as compelling (it doesn't for reasons I will explain later), Lennon's idealism now seems trite and ho-hum. The lyrics sound too much like a beauty pageant contestant who gets up on stage and explains her sincere belief in our need for world peace. The theme just doesn't have teeth.

The book you're about to read has been written in response to a new song, a song with teeth. It's not a song that you would hear on any Top 40 station or, in fact, any music station, but it is a song you might hear on National Public Radio or the BBC. Actually, it's not a song at all. But it is a message, in some ways not too different from Lennon's. The message goes something like this:

Imagine there're no credible words of Jesus.
It's easy if you try.
No sustaining evidence below us,
Above us only sky.

The singer of this "song" is Bart D. Ehrman; the name of his CD, *Misquoting Jesus: The Story Behind Who Changed the Bible and Why*. In this *New York Times* best-selling book, Ehrman claims that the changes to the textual tradition of the New Testament are so numerous and so profound that we can no longer speak meaningfully about getting back to the words and actions of the real Jesus. In other words, because the Bible is dependent on ancient manuscripts, and because these manuscripts are so thoroughly corrupt, we in essence no longer have Jesus: he has been lost in transmission.

The important difference between Lennon's ditty and Ehrman's thesis is that while the former claims only to be conveying his personal philosophy, the latter claims to be delving into history. The first asks us to imagine; the second tells us that this is the way it is and was. Whatever Jesus said, whatever the authors of Matthew, Mark, Luke, and John wrote, the truth of the matter is that we no longer have access to the original words. They have been lost in the black hole of history, and we can demonstrate this, Ehrman says, by examining history.

As for Lennon's song, you can take it or leave it. But when it comes to history, the stakes are staggeringly higher. If utopian visions have to do with what we can be, history has to do with what we have been. It is history that defines us. If Christianity is based on the teachings of Jesus, it would be quite embarrassing for Christians if it turned out that what were thought to be Jesus' teachings were not his teachings at all.

And so it appears that the followers of Jesus, at least those followers who understand the written words of Jesus as being his true words, are faced with a decision. They have basically three choices: (1) concede the force of Ehrman's argument, (2) offer a counter to Ehrman's argument, or (3) ignore the whole matter and hope that this unsettling talk about changes to the manuscript tradition goes away. In my mind, the worst of these options is number three. And yet, in surveying the past performance of conservative Christians in the face of challenge, I find that option number three seems to have been a kind of instinctive default mode. When issues like this have come up over the years, conservative Christianity has had an unfortunate track record of putting its head in the sand. This has been documented historically.[1]

This state of affairs reminds me of a passage, not from the Bible or a biblical prophet, but from a different kind of prophet, one of my dead, high school mentors whom I read alongside my favorite gospel writer: Friedrich Nietzsche (1844–1900). In *The Gay Science*, Nietzsche recounts a parable in which a madman runs into the village square. His message: God is dead. "God is dead. God remains dead," he rants, "and we have killed him." The people gather around this curiosity and laugh. "God is dead? How can God be dead? We all go to church," they seem to be saying. They laugh because they think the madman is nothing more than a harmless lunatic. They go on with their lives, only eventually to come to the realization, slowly and reluctantly, that the madman, who stands for Nietzsche himself, may be right.

From the Christian point of view, Nietzsche may be interpreted as having thrown down the gauntlet: unless Western Christianity would come to terms with the cultural changes that Nietzsche saw on the horizon, it would surely die a slow death. In part, especially in post-Christian Europe, Nietzsche and his madman have been proved right. Because Christians have had lapses of intellectual courage to deal with ideas or cultural currents that have challenged the way Christianity has traditionally looked at things, their movement has suffered all the more for it. Today's madman is often tomorrow's prophet, and the next day's purveyor of obvious truisms. Had Nietzsche's townspeople had the foresight, had the late nineteenth-century church known better, they would have invited the madman in for a meal, taken the time to understand what he was saying, weighed the matter, then wrestled with it.

For centuries Christians have trusted their Bibles as the inspired Word of God. But now along comes an all-too-reasonable-sounding "madman" (although certainly not the first, as shall become clear) with a story to tell. In the introduction of his book, Ehrman shares how he, having grown up in a church setting, had a conversion experience as a teenager. After attending Moody Bible Institute then moving on to Wheaton (my present stomping ground where I now teach New Testament), Ehrman began to harbor doubts about the reliability of Scripture. He reports that while undertaking doctoral work at Princeton, he took a class on his favorite gospel, the gospel of Mark. He wrote a paper in which he sought to address the problem as to why Abiathar is named as the high priest in Mark 2:26, while the account of 1 Samuel 21 clearly states that the high priest at the time was Ahimelech. After turning in this paper, which included an elaborate explanation as to why Mark had it right after all, Ehrman finally received it back from his professor, along with this comment tucked away in the margin: "Maybe Mark just made a mistake."[2]

For Ehrman that changed everything. There was a time when he, like evangelicals today, believed in something called plenary, verbal inspiration, the idea that God inspired every last word of Scripture. But if plenary, verbal inspiration is true, he reasoned, then that also means that every last word must be factually accurate. Ehrman's struggle with an apparent inaccuracy in Mark (the gospel writer's muffing the name of the high priest) meant the end of believing in Scripture as God-breathed. The protective barrier of the doctrine of verbal inspiration could no longer keep out the raging waters of textual contradictions. And unlike the little boy keeping his finger in the dike, Ehrman believed that he found a hole too big for his finger. Better to walk away and let the floodwaters take their course. Today, Ehrman declares himself to be a firmly convinced agnostic, and perhaps he would say that this is because the floodwaters have taken their course. There is, I am sure, more to his story than that—there always is. But the story itself is in its own way compelling.

Presumably, Ehrman's newfound view that the gospel writers fiddled with the facts gave him permission to think of the scribes as also messing around—in pretty fundamental ways—with the biblical tradition as they went about their task. To be sure, this is a provocative thesis and nothing to dismiss lightly. If Ehrman is the "madman" within the narthex of the conservative church,

Christians might with a nervous chuckle show him to the doorway of their minds, but the truth of the matter is that he is not going away—at least not that easily.

Besides, Christians should remember what's at stake. If following Jesus means anything, it means living a life of integrity and therefore also a life that steadily refuses to participate in the obstruction of truth. But people can be tempted to suppress the truth when they feel something precious will be lost if the truth comes out. That is why, in the trafficking of ideas, we must be wary of the faux pearl of great price, the sense of stability that accompanies the delusive conviction that we have thoroughly and decisively made sense of the world. When people succumb to that temptation of ignoring challenges to their faith, they are in the end demonstrating that they are more committed to the feeling of having a lock on truth than they are to truth itself. When Christians succumb to the same temptation, there is the added temptation of justifying their intellectual disengagement by appealing to faith or the Holy Spirit or something like that. Not only does this rationale shut down a discussion that is probably worth having; it also usually has more to do with intellectual laziness or megalomania than anything remotely biblical or divine. No one should be readier than the Christian to explore the truth (as Nietzsche himself rightly pointed out elsewhere in his writings); no one should be quicker to say, "We need to have a discussion about this."

As it turns out, the discussion that *Misquoting Jesus* prompts is part of a much larger and long-standing conversation. Like Lennon in his song "Imagine," Bart Ehrman is an author who is saying nothing entirely new; like Lennon again, he is taking his place in a chorus that has been performing since the Enlightenment. Ehrman writes as one who is particularly concerned with the discipline of textual criticism, the reconstruction of the biblical autographs—that is, the original manuscripts penned or dictated by the biblical writers themselves. As a leading authority on this subject, he deserves to be heard. But when we ask about what we can know and not know about the words of Jesus, it should come as no surprise that there's more to it than text-critical considerations. There are other issues dealing with the documentation of Jesus' life and words that are equally, if not more, important. We might call this Jesus scholarship.

The results of more than two centuries of Jesus scholarship have been mixed. Some have been saying that we can know a good deal about what Jesus said and did; others are far less sanguine. Such disagreement can be disconcerting. Why does one set of scholars say one thing and another set something very different? Is there any hope of sorting through these issues ourselves? What can we actually say about the words of Jesus? Do we have them in our Bibles or not? If we do have them in our Bibles, why don't we have other gospels (the ancient *Gospel of Thomas*, for example) in our Bibles as well? Moreover, what about the broad range of English translations? Can they all be so different and yet be so accurate? These are all good questions. They deserve answers.

I have written this book for two categories of people. First of all, I have written this book for the nonreligious person who has at least some passing interest in Jesus. There are more than a few in this category. Year in and year out, Jesus remains a hot news item. He never fails to make the cover of some major newsmagazine and never fails to pique the interest of American life and culture. Jesus is not just a matter of church discussion; a lot has been said and will continue to be said about Jesus in the public arena.

Unfortunately, those who write and speak authoritatively on Jesus are not always up front with their own methodological assumptions. Nor are they always forthcoming with the fact that these assumptions are in turn driven by prior faith decisions. I don't mind this so much. Who am I, one who has made faith decisions of my own, to begrudge other scholars their faith decisions? What I do mind, however, is when these same scholars pretend that they are approaching their material from some objective and scientific vantage point. In our day and age, the presentation of objective and "pure history," implied in a certain scientific style of writing, is now readier than ever to be seen for what it is. Rules for doing Jesus scholarship don't just materialize out of thin air: someone—someone who wants to win the game—makes the rules.

The uninformed non-Christian walking into the parlor for the first time deserves at least a passing glimpse into what the rules are and who made them. Before the non-Christian makes up his or her mind about Jesus, to the extent that contemporary scholarship on the words of Jesus weighs into the reasoning process, he or she should have a grip on the big picture. After all, if you are where I was some twenty-five years ago, if you are contemplating giving your life to following one whose only surviving words are now subject to serious question, it makes sense to find out what the questioning is all about.

I have also written this book for the church. A number of unsettling things are being said about Jesus, things that, one would suppose, every thinking Christian is obliged to work through. If the claims of Ehrman and others are really true, this will mean a major rethink for millions of devout believers. But if they are not true, how do we know they are not true? What is the basis for the claim that Jesus' words have been lost in transmission? What is the basis for the claim that they have been preserved?

These questions must be raised and must, in some manner, be resolved. It will not do simply to say that Ehrman is a dreamer, because, the fact of the matter is, he's not the only one. He hopes, I'm sure, that someday many will join him in his views. Many already have and presumably too many will.

I believe that there is a better route to take. It is a path that involves, in the first seven chapters, sorting out our presuppositions about Jesus: what was true of Jesus, what do people *wish* were true of Jesus, and how do these two considerations together radically affect the historical reconstruction of the words of Jesus? In order to understand the results of Jesus scholarship, you have to understand the worldviews and assumptions that have driven that scholarship. In other words, you have to understand how the rules became the rules. I maintain here that for the better part of the past three centuries, Jesus scholarship has generally overlooked Jesus' identity as a Jew and has therefore undervalued the historical value of his words. By doing justice to history, by restoring Jesus to Judaism, we see that his recorded words in fact acquire a high degree of reliability. If we change the rules as they need to be changed, this will also change the score considerably.

In the remaining four chapters and conclusion, I turn to some of the particulars of Ehrman's argument and seek to discuss in an intellectually responsible way what we can and can't know about the words of Jesus. There are many steps from Jesus to eyewitnesses, from eyewitnesses to autograph gospels, from autograph gospels to copies of the same, from copies to a critical text, and finally to English translation. Here we begin by applying historical imagination to the past (as every historian must do) then finally conclude by applying theological imagination to the present and future. If, as I am hoping to make clear throughout this book, Jesus scholarship inevitably involves issues of belief (theology), I cannot help but talk about theology, though I save this for the conclusion.

The reliability of Jesus' words is no trivial matter, for in the Gospels, including the gospel of Mark, we have Jesus making some extremely strong claims. The Gospels themselves report on Jesus' vision for the whole world: that one day creation would be one under his lordship. If this report is basically right, then the world has to reckon with this Jesus. But if this report is basically wrong, if Christendom has egregiously misquoted Jesus, then the world can go on its way while modern-day Christians may find that their next best option is falling back on the dreamy world proposed by Lennon. If you can imagine the church capitulating to the Enlightenment narrative in which God has not spoken, then you can imagine what's at stake in the claim that Jesus has been lost in transmission. It's not hard to do.

ONE

LOST IN TRANSMISSION?

The Bible began to appear to me as a very human book. Just as human scribes had copied, and changed, the texts of scripture, so too had human authors *written* the texts of scripture. . . . Many of these authors no doubt felt they were inspired by God to say what they did, but they had their own perspectives, their own beliefs, their own views, their own needs, their own desires, their own understanding, their own theologies; and these perspectives, beliefs, views, needs, desires, understanding, and theologies informed everything they said. . . . Occasionally I see a bumper sticker that reads: "God said it, I believe it, and that settles it." My response is always, 'What if God didn't say it? What if the book you take as giving you God's words instead contains human words?"

—BART EHRMAN, *Misquoting Jesus*

Dinner!"

It was evening and my wife and I were bustling around in the kitchen, putting the plates on the table, filling the glasses with ice, getting the silverware and napkins out. Everything was just about ready. A few minutes passed.

"Dinner!" The call went out again, this time with a little more force and urgency, even irritation. Now the steam was rolling off of the open dishes that were by this time set out on the table. We were short one family member, one who happened to have his friend over.

Finally, I got up from the table, walked into the next room, and found two boys deeply engrossed in a video game with zombie-like concentration. I told the one boy it was time for him to go. I told the other it was time for dinner. On the way back to the kitchen, I asked, "We have already called you twice. Why didn't you come?"

"I didn't hear you," he said.

Apparently, something was lost in transmission. There was only one thing to say: "Mmmm."

Lost in transmission. It can be a powerful defense. As any lawyer knows, there is no such thing as a binding contract unless there has been a successful meeting of the minds. If it can proved that the terms of the contract were ambiguously conveyed, then the contract itself can be invalidated. To the young woman receiving an unwanted cell phone call from an ex-boyfriend, the sound of a bad connection is a sweet one. "Hello? . . . Hello? . . . I'm losing you. . . . We might as well hang up" means the end of conversation and, if all things go as she intends, maybe even the final conversation. When Neil Armstrong was accused of botching his line when stepping onto the lunar surface for the first time (saying, "One small step for man, one giant leap for mankind," instead of "One small step for *a* man, one giant leap for mankind"), NASA defended its man on the moon by claiming that the sound of "a" was lost to outer space.

For better or for worse, rightly or wrongly, the claim of "lost in transmission" has the power of putting us in the clear. It declares that the attempt toward communication was abortive. The unsuccessful transfer of ideas is like a tree that falls in the forest. Sure, it might make a sound. But if the human ear does not pick up on the sound with at least some recognition, what difference does it make? Human communication demands a closed loop, and when the loop is demonstrably still open, all bets are off.

This is because communication is intrinsic to relationship. We all have known marriages—maybe you feel you're part of one—that involve poor communication. Such marriages tend to be difficult. The communication of one's hopes, goals, intentions, fears, memories, expectations, perceptions, judgments, joys—all these contribute to strengthening and rejuvenating the marital relationship. But without such communication, the partners each lose a sense of the other and they slowly drift apart. Eventually, the only thing left on the horizon is the isolated self. Interpersonal relationship is ultimately impossible without communication.

But in some cases there is something appealing about failure in communication. More precisely, sometimes we *want* communication to fail, when we as receivers realize that the content of the communication is potentially burdensome or disturbing. This is true when it comes to knowing things and knowing people. Some mail you open right away; other mail, like the credit card bill, you leave unopened for a few days, maybe a few weeks. Sometimes you just don't want to know because you don't want to be disturbed. The same can apply to interpersonal communication. Whatever it was that someone was hoping, expecting, or demanding that you do or be, the lost-in-transmission plea is a virtual guarantee of absolution from obligation or guilt. After all, no one can expect you to fulfill a request that never really registered with you. And so you can go on free as a bird with your good name, clear conscience, and personal agenda unruffled.

Of course the Christian claim that the God of Israel has revealed himself to the world through Jesus Christ can be profoundly disturbing, deeply unsettling. Had orthodox Christianity asked us to deal only with the deist god, a far-away god who got creation started but whom we haven't heard from since, we would be dealing with a god who ultimately gives nothing to us and asks nothing from us. Or had Christianity called us to imagine a god who was so closely identified with creation that he or she became creation itself, including ourselves, this god, too, could not be capable of a personal relationship. Nor can the romantic and existential god-as-Infinite-Being bear the burden and promise of a meaningful interpersonal interchange. Such gods could not communicate in a way that would bear even remote analogy to human communication. The god of deism, the god of pantheism, even the god of philosophical existentialism—such gods are hardly disturbing at all. Such gods do not require that we be in contact with them. In fact, interpersonal communication with these gods is in the nature of the case impossible. But if the god revealed by Jesus Christ is the true god (that is, God), this means that the Creator is a personal God and has in fact initiated a kind of relationship with humanity that obliges all people everywhere to respond with their lives.

This was beginning to dawn on me very early on in my first reading of Mark. In the first verse we read: "The beginning of the gospel of Jesus Christ, the Son of God." Fifteen verses into this gospel, we find Jesus saying: "The kingdom of God is at hand. Repent, and believe in the gospel." For me there was something both inviting and scandalous about this proclamation. Jesus' reference to a spiritual reality was strangely comforting because it was outside of and bigger than myself. Yet—and here is where the scandal comes in—if this kingdom transcends me and my interests, then this same kingdom also likely will involve my deferring to that transcendent reality at different points, perhaps even on an ongoing basis. Jesus' choice of metaphor, the *kingdom* of God, sounded so all-encompassing. It suggested that to be involved with this kingdom meant subordinating one's life to this exterior reality. If I were to follow through, it would mean the end of me as I have known me.

There's no getting around the fact that every relationship has its own terms and conditions. Your friends, family, coworkers, and other relations might not necessarily spell out those terms explicitly, but there are terms. Every relationship has its own boundaries as to what goes and what doesn't go. I realize today that it's no different with God's relationship with humanity. I realize, too, that in my first take on Mark's gospel I was right about the demanding nature of Jesus' kingdom invitation, more right than I knew. If Jesus Christ was truly who he claimed to be, if Jesus Christ was truly what his first followers claimed him to be, this has very weighty implications that impose themselves on every human individual. Deism (the belief that god is far away and isn't about to come back) and pantheism (the belief that god physically indwells everything everywhere) limit the freedom of god but preserve the absolute freedom of the human person. Such an arrangement, where god is constrained and we are free, does not approach the human-divine relationship portrayed in Scripture. When god is equated with an "intimation of immortality" (Wordsworth) or a "feeling of absolute dependence" (Schleiermacher), this may leave room for awe of the holy or the thrill of mystical escape, but this, too, should not be confused with the God who is revealed in Jesus Christ.

What the God behind the gospel of Mark was requiring was— if I had the word for it at the time—worship. And by this term I do not mean simply the act of going to church. Worship, biblical worship, is not only our way of responding to God's self-revelation but also our way of surrendering our very selves, even as the same God lays claim to us through revelation. The act of worship is the truest expression of our humanity. One is never more human than when one worships in response to God. If we do not sense this immediately, it is because something within us resists our coming to terms with our true humanity. The implications of the self-revelation of Jesus Christ do not necessarily make life more convenient for us as individuals, but at the time I was unwilling to entertain the possibility that God was seeking something more profound and long-lasting than my convenience.

Having used the term "revelation" a few times now, let me explain what I mean. When Christian theologians talk about revelation, they are usually talking about one of two things. In the first place, revelation refers to the "Christ-event": Jesus of Nazareth's appearance on the stage of history, what Jesus said and did in time and space. This is the Jesus as he actually was, the Jesus whose image and voice, had you a video camera, could have been caught on tape and preserved for all of posterity. Scholars call this Jesus the "historical Jesus" or the "pre-Easter Jesus."

But revelation also refers to what his followers under inspiration wrote down of what he said and did. This is not the flesh-and-blood Jesus but the church's description of the flesh-and-blood Jesus. It is important to distinguish between the two. I would never deny that a picture of me wasn't "me." But a picture of a person is not the same thing as the person's self; it is instead a visual representation. The same goes for the Gospels (Matthew, Mark, Luke, and John): they are literary representations of Jesus.

One of the more interesting implications of this dead-obvious fact is that the gospel accounts of Jesus cannot claim to be exhaustive. In fact, when John says that even the whole world would not contain the books that could be written about the deeds of Jesus, he underscores that his story of Jesus is a limited, selective story (John 21:25). When you are selective, as any biographer or historian must be, this entails a certain degree of interpretation. What to include? What to leave out? These are the sorts of questions tied up with one's interpretation of one's subject. Thus, it would be foolish to argue that the four gospels are anything less than interpretations of Jesus. Scholars call the Jesus depicted in these interpretive accounts the "Christ of faith" or the "post-Easter Jesus."

But it would be a grave mistake to surmise, as many do at this point, that interpretative accounts—because they are *interpretive*—play fast and loose with the facts of history. To imagine that objective historiography (history writing) and interpretive historiography are mutually exclusive undertakings is to fall into the illusion that the facts of history speak for themselves. But do they really? And if they do, where do they speak for themselves? Where do we find purely objective history?

Do we find such objectivity in the classical historiographers like Thucydides? Hardly. Thucydides would have winced at the thought that he should have written his account of the Peloponnesian War as if he were an aloof spectator. What about modern historical treatments such as Barbara W. Tuchman's *A Distant Mirror* (Knopf, 1978) or Bruce Catton's *Grant Takes Command* (Little, Brown and Company, 1969)? Are these purely objective? They may be balanced, but they cannot be said to be objective. What thinking and feeling soul can begin to write a history of the papal schism or the American Civil War without certain assumptions and prior value judgments regarding each of those events? What about television media reports on domestic or international happenings? Shouldn't these journalists strive as professionals to tell the story without any trace of interpretive bias? If you think so, you should probably seriously consider disconnecting your cable or satellite dish.

At the end of the day, it is impossible to contemplate the recollection of past or contemporary events without the selection, orientation, organization, and representation of those events somehow coloring or interpreting the facts. To observe is to interpret; to observe out loud is to interpret out loud. There is no such thing as interpretation-free history. Balance is a fine ideal, but purely objective history, something else entirely, is an illusion.

Therefore, there should be no embarrassment or backwardness in affirming that the gospel writers in a very human way interpreted the Jesus they were writing about. After all, the only thinking being who can get away with not interpreting reality is God himself. The gospel writers knew they were interpreting Jesus, and I believe that they rejoiced in this fact. Much as a painter rejoices because his or her medium is able to convey a certain impression that other media (portrait photography, for example) cannot, so, too, I suspect that the gospel writers, fully aware that they were approaching their subject from different angles, exulted in the variety of their takes on Jesus. The fact that the canonical gospels are four in number and not just one doesn't impoverish our understanding of Jesus. Rather, it enriches it.

The gospel writers also knew that they were writing with specific purposes in mind. Of course, when you think about it, you probably wouldn't want it any other way. (Have you ever caught a college professor talking about that great student paper that also happened to be written with no perceivable purpose in mind? I don't think so.) At times, the gospel writers are less than explicit in conveying their purpose; at other points, they are more so. John mentions that he writes his gospel "that you may believe" (John 20:31). Luke writes his gospel for Theophilus, "that you may know the certainty of those things in which you were instructed" (Luke 1:4). The gospel writers are no disinterested parties. Their relationship to their focal interest is anything but dispassionate, detached, or casual. The Jesus they write about is the Jesus they want us to believe and embrace.

This point, which is hard to miss, has been the source of stumbling for many a New Testament scholar. Such scholars read the New Testament and conclude that the biblical authors' theological agenda—their "beliefs, views, needs, desires"—was overwhelming inducement either to distort the facts or, less self-consciously, to be lax regarding the truthfulness of their report. Like the desperate preacher inventing an illustration allegedly drawn from personal experience, the first Jesus storytellers are thought to sacrifice the facts of the matter on the altar of a good homiletic story.

For many who see the Gospels this way, the absence of historical factuality does serious damage to the theological value of their message. For others, the perception of compromised historical accuracy does not detract from the writing's theological significance in the least. On the contrary, they might say, to treat the Gospels as history is to distract from what the ancient writers were trying to do: "Of course the New Testament writers were not attempting to write history. They were *theologians*, for goodness' sake!" In either case, the unspoken assumption is that homiletics (writing a good sermon) and history (getting the facts right) are mutually exclusive endeavors. Since the biblical writers had theological goals, we are told, they cannot be trusted as reliable conveyors of the Jesus tradition.

But there is, as I'm hoping to make clear, a fallacy at the heart of this thinking. I have already made the point that the opposition between objective reportage and interpretation is a false one. If this is true, then it quickly becomes apparent that playing the historian against the theologian is a move that just doesn't work. There is no reason to reject the possibility that the gospel writers were attempting to wear two hats simultaneously and to wear them well.

There is a regular correlate to this odd splitting apart of history and theology. As I have already mentioned, we can understand revelation in two senses. Jesus Christ himself can be considered the living, breathing, eating, sleeping, 24/7 revelation of God (John 1:1; Heb. 1:1–4). But revelation refers not only to the person of Jesus but also to the story about Jesus, as set down in the New Testament gospels. Generally speaking, those who see the gospel writers as theologians rather than historians (instead of entertaining the possibility of both being true) see the gospel accounts as revelation only in a derivative and secondary sense. Jesus is the real deal, but as for the gospel writers . . . "Well, they try." And one of the main things that trips them up is their all-too-human agenda. For these readers of the New Testament, it seems that Jesus is about one thing and the early church about something altogether different. For these readers, too, Christianity is not about what the canonical writers say about this or that; it's about getting past the distorting influences of the earliest writers or witnesses and getting back to the *real* Jesus, who, when you get right down to it, is either alone the revelation of God or the one mortal who had extraordinary access to the life of God.

But this does not seem to be how the early church thought about it. Moreover, it may be argued that the canonical gospels (Matthew, Mark, Luke, and John), and in fact the New Testament canon as a whole, have a deeper revelatory significance than Jesus himself. Whatever you believe about Jesus' life, death, and resurrection, one thing is for certain: the historical Jesus has come and gone, and he has left no immediate material traces of himself. He never wrote a book, he never left us the Sermon on the Mount on DVD, and he never gave a tape-recorded interview. Those who knew Jesus personally or recognized him on the street knew the historical Jesus. But we, those living today along with the vast majority of Christians down through the ages, have no direct access to the historical Jesus. For our purposes, the *only* revelation we have is the revelation contained in the canonical gospels. True enough, these revelatory documents point to another revelation that preceded them. But if revelation requires a transaction between the knower (in this case, you or me) and that which is known (in this case, Jesus), then revelation of Jesus comes most fully into its own through the New Testament stories about Jesus. If Jesus is who orthodox Christianity says he is, then it appears that Jesus' appointed means for revealing himself to the church of the succeeding ages are the human, all too human, Scriptures. When it comes to transmitting what Jesus said and did, the fourfold gospel ultimately provides the only window we have. Therefore, as far as the God of Christian orthodoxy seems to be concerned, it is the only record we need.

But how translucent is this window? How accurate and clear is the view the gospel writers gave us? For the vast majority of church history, most interpreters peering through the Gospels to the history of Christian origins have said that the view is very clear. But beginning with the Enlightenment, interpreters began to say, "No, actually the view is not clear at all." The ensuing conflict, between those who were confident that Jesus' words could be recouped and those who were equally confident that they could not, has set the stage for our discussion today.

For our purposes, we want to narrow the question: have Jesus' words been lost in transmission or not? In asking this, we must confess from the start that this particular issue cannot be honestly treated without some recognition of the presuppositions driving the modern-day historians of Jesus. In the remaining chapters of this first part of this book, I will discuss some of these presuppositions more thoroughly.

For now, it is enough to point out how Ehrman criticizes the orthodox view of revelation by smuggling in theological concepts that are inherently at odds with the orthodox belief structure. First, Ehrman sets up a dilemma that goes as follows: either the Bible contains the words of God, or it contains human words. Given the choice between the two, Ehrman decides that the Bible contains human words. But putting it this way misses the point. No right-thinking Christian would ever deny that the Bible contains human words. Of course the Bible contains human words. After all, Paul, Mark, and the rest were not from Mars. The proper question is whether the words of Scripture are, on analogy with Jesus Christ himself, fully human *and* fully divine.

Apparently, as Ehrman sees it, the fact that the gospel writers' "perspectives, beliefs, views, needs, desires, understanding, and theologies informed everything they said" underscores the humanity and invalidates the divinity of their writings. But this presumes that

God and humanity can never meet. This presumes, too, that God's hands are tied when it comes to speaking through human subjectivity; it decides ahead of time that the biblical writers' perceptions and motivations make for an insurmountable obstacle for truth. But if we are going to gauge the Bible's truthfulness, we should do so not by importing—as Ehrman does—some Platonic idealism (which sees truth as some kind of objective, free-floating abstraction out there somewhere), but by using the Bible's own definition of truth: Jesus Christ himself. The incarnation informs us that truth not only can take on human form, but in order to be true truth, it *must* take on human form. The Bible is indeed a fully human document. God in his wisdom would not have had it any other way. But this human dimension does not mean that the original voice behind the text has been lost in transmission; nor does it rule out the possibility that the Scriptures are also fully divine. To criticize the traditional Christian doctrine of inspiration on the basis of a Platonic philosophy of knowledge seems to me like installing a lawn mower spark plug in your Toyota then complaining to the dealership when it doesn't start.

Shaky theology on this point, however, does not invalidate the historical question lingering behind Ehrman's remarks, quoted at the beginning of this chapter. On the contrary, when Jesus says, "Repent, for the kingdom of God is at hand," we have to decide for ourselves whether we actually have Jesus' words here or only the words that Mark put in Jesus' mouth. Have Jesus' words been overwritten? Have they been lost in transmission?

Again, there has been a difference of opinion on the matter. But maybe we are getting slightly ahead of ourselves. In sorting through the "knowability" of Jesus' words, perhaps the very first thing we need to decide is whether the question is in fact moot, for a number of recent writers have been claiming that Jesus never even existed. Is there any substance to this claim? You will have to decide for yourself after reading the next chapter.

TWO

DID JESUS LIVE?

Christians, of course, were eager to know more about the
life, teachings, death, and resurrection of their Lord and
so numerous Gospels were written, which recorded the
traditions associated with the life of Jesus.

—BART EHRMAN, *Misquoting Jesus*

But with all due respect, sir," the young man protested, "Jesus never existed."

I had just completed a public evening lecture on the historical Jesus at a nearby university. Moments after summarizing my thoughts and receiving the audience's polite applause, I opened the floor for questions. I had not even finished doing so when an undergraduate put up his hand. He was sitting in the center of the front row. His arm went up so quickly and so decisively that it would have been impossible for me not to have noticed him first. We've all had the experience of a student in a class or a member of a lecture audience making a statement that only pretended to be a question. But there was no pretense here, for here there was not even a hint of a question. It was all statement: the historical Jesus was a figment of someone's imagination, and successive generations have fallen for a literary fabrication. As far as this young man was concerned, Jesus did not exist any more than the Marlboro Man or Wonder Woman.

I'm not sure, but I think I smiled at the time. Not because I thought it was a silly statement, but because for a moment, through his expression of earnestness, impetuousness, and defiance, I saw a familiar sight. I saw myself. If I smiled, it was not a condescending smile. It was a smile that well remembered the inner tension of being unsettled by God.

Back in my sophomore year of high school, in Mr. Heath's English class, we were assigned to read J. D. Salinger's *Catcher in the Rye*, a standard high school novel, set in the 1950s. It's about a young man named Holden Caufield who was on a journey in search of himself and of that which was not "phony." When you're a teen, you're just undertaking the process of forming a self-identity, which in turn requires you to decide what counts and what doesn't in life, what's real and what's not. You come to realize that actually there's a lot of phoniness out there. You begin to see through things, just as in a few years' time my children will begin—and already have begun—to see right through me and my inconsistencies.

The teenage years are also the years when you begin to think critically, when you begin to discover that the assured certainties of life are not quite as certain as you have been led to believe. You learn to think independently, and at points, in order to assert that independence, you often take your stand against certain received truths. After starting to read Mark, I began to wonder whether this world I had known, a world without a God who speaks, was actually a myth of somebody's devising. It was the first time I was at the fence of the conceptual playground in which I had spent my young life, and I was seriously wondering what was on the other side.

Even if this young man may have been looking from the opposite direction, I sensed that he had come to the very same fence. If

I were to guess, I would say that he grew up in the church and then, after reading this or that, came to be persuaded that the whole thing was a myth devised by early Christians. For many of us, especially when we feel as though we're on the verge of busting a life-long myth, a deep inner ambivalence drives us to climb the fence and either taunt those on the other side or glare back on the convictions we have known and shake our fist violently. For a time we may become ardent evangelists for our momentary conviction, whether it be that God is dead or alive. We may even possibly take our shot at playing the role of Nietzsche's madman, again either for or against God, but we have not necessarily settled ourselves. The most formidable evangelist is the one who has, over the course of time, allowed his or her convictions to seep into his or her life, causing that life to attain a certain inexorable beauty. However, it also needs to be said that while all worldviews lead somewhere, not all worldviews lead to beauty.

Despite my twinge of sympathy with this young man who disagreed with just about everything I had to say about Jesus, I was taken aback by his statement. Given the number of people there, I would have thought the chances of finding anyone in the audience who disbelieved Jesus' existence would have been very slim indeed. Maybe I'm naïve. Maybe I don't get out enough. But, then again, that night I was guest to an institution that, much to its chagrin, was home to a notorious tenured professor who claimed that the Holocaust was a hoax. Was this a copycat effect among those who hold to strange conspiracy theories? Still, a sincerely stated conviction deserves a respectful and well-reasoned answer.

My best answer goes something like this: anyone seeking to deny the historical Jesus is attempting something that is at once too difficult and too easy. It is too difficult in that the evidence for the existence of Jesus is so strong; were we to reject it, it would ultimately mean either glaring inconsistencies between our approach to Jesus history and our approach to other kinds of history or that virtually nothing can be said about history at all. The denial of Jesus is too easy in that it relieves us from the labor of tackling a much thornier question: who was Jesus? Intellectual abdication and methodological inconsistency, or intellectual abdication and a minimalism amounting to nihilism: this young man, like all deniers of the historical Jesus, must take his pick.

The nonexistence of Jesus is not a novel idea; it has come and gone a few times in the past several hundred years. In the late eighteenth century, C. F. Volney proposed that Jesus was developed on the basis of the sun god. Fifty years later, Bruno Bauer wrote *Christianity Exposed* (1843), a work that built on his thesis that the figure of Jesus was an idealization of philosophical concepts. Roughly another half century after that, Arthur Drews' *The Christ Myth* (1911) put forth the idea that the Gospels were simply early Christian reflection on Old Testament scriptures, a notion that at least one contemporary Jesus scholar picks up on in his explanation of the resurrection accounts.[1]

Recent years have seen books on Jesus' nonexistence selling more than ever, as can be witnessed by G. A. Wells' *The Jesus Myth* (Open Court, 1998), Timothy Freke and Peter Gandy's *The Jesus Mysteries* (Harmony, 2000), and Earl Doherty's *The Jesus Puzzle* (Canadian Humanist, 1999). Each book, by its own line of argument, seeks to disprove Jesus. From a publisher's point of view, it is not hard to see the marketing prospects. Anyone setting out to write a book about "the Jesus who never was" is asking for controversy. And, as they say, there is no such thing as "bad press." Never mind the facts of history—outrageous ideas sell.

This is not to say that authors like Wells, Doherty, Freke, or Gandy were writing simply for mercenary reasons. No, I believe that these authors really believe what they are writing and really hope to convince their readers. Like Matthew, Mark, Luke, and John, who wrote their gospels because they were very much interested in commending the hero of their stories, these authors, too, have a dog in the Jesus fight. And rather than nipping at the heels, these writers go right for the jugular. Remove the historical Jesus from the body of the church altogether, and you have drained the lifeblood from Christianity.

Because space forbids my dealing with all the authors who have at one time or another denied Jesus' existence, and because most of these writers have been refuted very effectively elsewhere,[2] I will limit myself to one of the most recent arguments set forth in a book by Freke and Gandy; its full title is *The Jesus Mysteries: Was the "Original Jesus" a Pagan God?* Admittedly, in dealing only with this book, I am neglecting the specific arguments of other Jesus-deniers. So, while not taking the time to answer these authors comprehensively point by point, I hope that by singling out one of the most recent examples of this genre, I can illustrate that the arguments against Jesus' existence, at least to date, are not very strong after all.

The basic idea of *The Jesus Mysteries* is that Jesus was a mythological construct, a literary patchwork of various ancient gods, including Attis and Mithras, who were fused into the figure of Osiris-Dionysus. Like Jesus, the god-man Osiris-Dionysus is called "Savior" and "Son of God." He descends into hell and rises again. His followers are initiated into his name through a kind of baptism. According to Freke and Gandy, the explanation for these and other such parallels is that the authors of the canonical gospels were Hellenized Jews who melded their Judaism with pagan mystery religions. When a later generation of believers took the Gospels at face value, there was a parting of ways between those who knew better, the Gnostics, and the "Literalists" who formed the Great Church. To be sure, at first blush, this provides a rather plausible explanation of Christian origins.

There are, however, a vast number of problems with Freke and Gandy's argument, some minor, others major. Let me start with a basic methodological issue. Experts in comparative religions will regularly advise extreme caution in inferring influence from parallels between two mythic or religious systems, and that for good reason. When reading the New Testament, we find images such as light, darkness, life, death, rebirth; we also find concepts such as vicarious redemption and personal identification with the divine. But it would be foolish to suppose that these images and ideas are uniquely Christian, for anyone who has done even a little reading in the primary sources of world religions will see that there is nothing peculiarly Christian at all about such terms and images, even if there was a distinctive Christian use of them. And so we realize soon enough that when Christian images are anticipated in non-Christian religious literature or art, it does not follow that the former is dependent on the latter. If Christianity is true, then we would expect Christianity to resonate with the deepest longings of humanity, using some of the very same imagery that humanity has latched onto in order to express those longings. Likewise, if the God of Christianity was interested in conveying himself in meaningful terms, it should come as little surprise that these terms include archetypal patterns and universal images.

Apparently, Freke and Gandy seem to believe that Christianity, in order to be historically credible, must be thoroughly unique and unprecedented. But Christianity has never claimed to be either. Rather, if the incarnation, God's taking on flesh, is our basic starting point, we would expect that the form of God's self-revelation would indeed show considerable continuity with and similarities to other, non-Christian ways of talking about the divine. In order for God to relate meaningfully to humanity, he must at least in some measure invite us to think of God in ways that we are already predisposed to think about him.

Leaving God out of it and restricting ourselves on a very human level to the biblical writers, we come to the same result. What makes more sense, we might ask—that the New Testament authors sought to speak about their experience of God through terms that were completely foreign to the religious mix of the day, or that these writers actually saw these very terms, when transposed into a new key, as a strategic means of communication? There is no doubt that early Christian talk about God derived more than a few of its central terms from paganism.[3] But if the early Christians were following in the footsteps of the incarnate Christ, why shouldn't this be the case?

My argument carries weight as long as the similarities between Christianity and the Greco-Roman religions are merely superficial. But what if there was a way, when comparing Christianity to the pagan mystery religions, of proving substantive dependence of the former on the latter? If there was, Freke and Gandy's argument would be much more powerful. But in order to prove "substantive dependence," you have to begin with the realization that religious systems, like languages, have their own logic or grammar that explains why things are the way they are. Religious systems are also much like stories. If you understand the story line, the whole, then you will be much more successful in fitting the details into that larger framework. But if you don't understand the story line, then your project is doomed to failure. Although Freke and Gandy adduce a generous number of parallels between Greek mystery religions and Christianity, their complete inattention to the different ways in which these terms or concepts functioned in their respective contexts—their failure to understand the grammar or story line of the pagan mysteries and early Christianity—leaves the book deeply flawed.

We might take, for example, the coauthors' claim that Jesus is called "Savior" and "Son of God" because he is modeled on an Egyptian god who goes by the same names. This argument, which is by the way an old one, is simply not convincing. It is true that Osiris (the Greeks called him Serapis) is called "Savior" and "Son of God." But if Osiris-Serapis was looked upon as the source of healing and the one who saved you from your diseases, it would have been odd for the Egyptians *not* to have called their god "Savior." What else might we hope and expect the Egyptians to call Osiris? And if the early Christians believed that Jesus saved them, would we not also expect the same epithet to be applied to Jesus?[4]

That Osiris is deemed the "Son of God" is nothing startling either. The Egyptians looked to the pharaohs as sons of God; Osiris and other gods also were called sons of God. There is even a sense in which humanity itself is deemed sons of God. As the famous Egyptologist Eric Hornung writes:

All men may be god's children from birth . . . or may prove by their actions that they are images of god; the man with knowledge is also said elsewhere to be a "likeness . . . of god" and sons "images" of their fathers; in these cases what is meant is not a simple similarity but a fundamental kinship of action, nature, and rank.[5]

Hornung is referring in this context to middle period texts (2100–1300 BC), but given the conservative nature of the ancient Egyptian religious perspective, his words could equally apply to the Egyptians of the pre-Christian Roman period. In traditional Christian thought, there has been only one "Son of God"; in ancient Egypt, "sons of God" were a dime a dozen.

Further problems arise for Freke and Gandy's argument on consideration of the fact that as the Egyptians of the Roman period wrote out their prayers to "Lord Osiris" or "Osiris the Savior" or "Osiris, Son of God," they were almost certainly coalescing the titles of their pharaoh, who at this point was the Roman emperor, with their own divinities, including Osiris. Long before Jesus was even born, Caesar Augustus is called "Savior," "Lord," and "Son of God." In his account of Jesus' birth, Luke is very much aware of this fact and indeed seeks to capitalize on it in order to show that while other pseudo-lords and pseudo-saviors have come and gone, including now the Roman principate, the true Son of God, Lord, and Savior has arrived in Jesus (Luke 2:11). Luke purposefully uses Augustus' ways of referring to himself in order to make a point aimed squarely at the emperor: "You are on your way out, and someone far greater is on his way in!" Presumably, other early Christians alongside Luke did the same. Thus, although the earliest Christians found their initial inspiration for using these terms in their Hebrew scriptures, they also self-consciously drew on a pool of terms that was stock political language in the first-century world. That Osirians did the same proves nothing about Osirian mysticism influencing Christianity.

So much for Jesus as the Osirian Son of God, but what about Osiris rising from the dead? Doesn't that show some kind of influence on Christianity, perhaps seminal influence? Actually, that Osiris experiences life from death also demonstrates nothing: a good many ancient religions have their heroes do the same, including Zoroastrianism. But what Freke and Gandy miss is what can easily be missed given a superficial acquaintance with what the Scriptures actually teach. Whereas Osirianism envisaged simply a recontinuation of earthly existence in the underworld (that's why the Egyptians went to such lengths to preserve the bodies of their great and their good), Christianity was unique in proclaiming the raising of an immortal and incorruptible body as part of a new creation. When Paul talks about resurrection in 1 Corinthians 15, he is talking about something radically different from that for which the Osirians hoped.[6] In this case, Paul's gospel promises something far more glorious than what the Egyptians were in their own way groping for. The apostle's story is altogether different.

What about Christian baptism? Are Freke and Gandy right to suppose, for example, that Paul's discussion of baptism in Romans 6 draws on the thought world of the mystery religions? Again, while Paul mentions death in connection with baptism, the baptism he discusses is a baptism into the name of Christ, not a reenactment of death as it seems to have been for the mystery cult initiates. If the believer's union with Christ through baptism also includes, by extension, coparticipation in Christ's death (Rom. 6:3), this still stands at variance with the pagan understanding of the water ritual that symbolized death itself. For Paul, baptism signaled forgiveness and release from death, not a direct reentering into death.[7] Although the similarities between Paul's doctrine of baptism and Graeco-Roman conceptions of water initiation drew the attention of many scholars of the early twentieth-century "history of religions" school, a closer reading of Paul shows that whatever comparisons are to be made between Osirianism and early Christian practice, they are in the end unconvincing.

How do we weigh the force of Freke and Gandy's argument? By way of analogy, imagine you are a friend to an author who has just finished reading a Dan Brown best seller. He flips the last page, closes the book, slams it on the table, and shouts, "Thief! Brown plagiarized my book. We must call my lawyer at once!" And so, trying to be the dutiful friend, you go along to the meeting with the lawyer, who, after preliminary chitchat, asks your author friend why he thinks that Brown lifted his material. He responds with great agitation: "Well, so many of the words match! Look here on my page 1. Do you see that there? The word 'considered'—Brown has exactly the same word on his page 231. And now look at my page 2. The word 'the' comes up *multiple* times in Brown's novel!" After a period of listening to your companion's very long list of parallels, the lawyer suddenly looks at his watch, rises to his feet, and interrupts: "My, look at the time. It has been good seeing you again. Listen, why don't I send you a bill for consultation and we'll just call it quits. Okay?" You and your stunned friend are quickly ushered out the door. He thought he had a winnable case. Apparently, it was not as winnable as he thought.

Likewise, Freke and Gandy's case is not the slam dunk they seem to think. It is not enough for one bringing charges of plagiarism to cite isolated parallels; there also must be the sense that the meaning, the structure, the story line of the two narratives somehow line up. You cannot prove the dependence of a Dan Brown novel on another novel on the grounds that many words match; the case can only begin to hope to be persuasive after you have taken the time to read and understand both novels. In short, Freke and Gandy are unable to do this because they have not demonstrated an understanding of the story lines of either Christianity or the mystery religions.

We might finally consider the words of Papias of Hierapolis. Papias's words are being quoted by Eusebius (AD 275–339) as handed down by Irenaeus (AD 130–202). In this passage, he seems to be reflecting back on his practice of the last decades of the first century:

> But I shall not hesitate also to put down for you along with my interpretations whatsoever things I have at any time learned carefully from the elders and carefully remembered, guaranteeing their truth. For I did not, like the multitude, take pleasure in those that speak much, but in those that teach the truth; not in those that relate strange commandments, but in those that deliver the commandments given by the Lord to faith, and springing from the truth itself.
>
> If, then, any one came, who had been a follower of the elders, I questioned him in regard to the words of the elders—what Andrew or what Peter said, or what was said by Philip, or by Thomas, or by James, or by John, or by Matthew, or by any other of the disciples of the Lord, and what things Aristion and the presbyter John, the disciples of the Lord, say. For I did not think that what was to be

gotten from the books would profit me as much as what came from the living and abiding voice.[8]

Wanting to interview those who knew the Lord directly, Papias is only two removes away from the historical Jesus. And when those who knew Jesus personally were in town, Papias made it his goal to seek them out and quiz them on what they knew about him. But what if, as the skeptics would say, Jesus did not exist? Either the elders were in perfect collusion as to what they were going to say about Jesus' words and deeds, or Papias is merely writing as one who is "in on it." And if Papias is part of what would have been becoming at that time a worldwide conspiracy, it must have been a *very* large conspiracy indeed.

And here is where I think we come to another major problem within the nonexistent-Jesus argument. If Jesus did not exist, how do we explain the countless hordes of people who lived so close to the alleged time of Jesus and yet firmly believed in his existence? Moreover, if Jesus did not exist, any first-century Galilean or citizen of Jerusalem would have had a pretty easy time confirming as much simply by asking around. And yet thousands of such people, again, according to our authors, believed in Jesus without any immediate reason for doing so and, despite obvious reasons for doubting, refused to validate their belief when they clearly had the ability to do so. Again, the only way to salvage this argument is to suggest that Jesus' existence was a ruse perpetuated by an absolutely massive conspiracy involving thousands of people sticking to the assigned story even to the point of death. By the same stretch of the imagination, we might as well say that the Holocaust was also a hoax.

This way of doing history might play for those with ears eager to cash out the results, but for everybody else this is simply nonsense. The very logic that tells us there was no Jesus is the same logic that pleads that there was no Holocaust. On such logic, history is no longer possible. It is no surprise then that there is *no* New Testament scholar drawing pay from a post who doubts the existence of Jesus. I know not one. His birth, life, and death in first-century Palestine have never been subject to serious question and, in all likelihood, never will be among those who are experts in the field. The existence of Jesus is a given.

THREE

HISTORY, FAITH, AND CERTITUDE

What if the Bible doesn't give a foolproof answer to the questions of the modern age—abortion, women's rights, gay rights, religious supremacy, Western-style democracy, and the like? What if we have to figure out how to live and what to believe on our own, without setting up the Bible as a false idol—or an oracle that gives us a direct line of communication with the Almighty? There are clear reasons for thinking that, in fact, the Bible is not this kind of inerrant guide to our lives: among other things, as I've been pointing out, in many places we . . . don't even know what the original words of the Bible actually were.

—BART EHRMAN, *Misquoting Jesus*

I remember how when I was a child, in the days before anyone really wondered about the ethics of circus animal training, I went to the circus. It was a three-ring circus, of course. The bright colors, the constant movement, the smell of the greasepaint, the roar of the crowd—all this was more than enough titillation for the senses. In a three-ring circus there are always three acts going on simultaneously. The lion tamer, the fire-eater, and the trapeze artist were all vying for attention as if his or her act was the only one that mattered, as if it was the only act under the canopy. Which ring do you pay more attention to, and to which do you pay less attention?

Under the big tent of those who write on Jesus, there is also a kind of three-ring circus. Each "ring" has its own specific set of performers; each act has its own attractions. Each act uses its own tools and has its own intentions. Sometimes the various acts go on almost as if they were oblivious to one another's existence. Sometimes, too, in the midst of the noise and confusion, the spectators are fooled into thinking that there is only one ring; they go home having watched only one of the three rings, not realizing that there is more to it than they were aware.

In due course we will be able to talk about Jesus' words. But we must first take a considerable preliminary step: we must understand who Jesus was. Unfortunately, this is no simple undertaking, for in approaching Jesus as the human object of historical inquiry, we are immediately confronted with the problem of our own subjectivity. For all of us, our thinking about God plays into the way we prefer to think of the historical Jesus, and vice versa. Our theology informs how we interpret history, and how we interpret history informs our theology. Given the nature of Jesus' claims, there is no way of avoiding this. Since the Enlightenment there have been basically three ways that people have correlated theology and history in their construal of Jesus. As a result, we have come to find ourselves in a three-ring circus.

The best way of describing these three rings is, I think, just to retell the story as it began to unfold in late eighteenth-century Germany. One might say that it all started with the posthumous publication of Hermann Samuel Reimarus's writings, the *Wolfenbüttel Fragments*. An academician specializing in Semitic studies, Reimarus (1694–1768) appeared to be a very devout man, one who even published a number of defenses of orthodox Christianity. At least that was his public image. But the private Reimarus, the Reimarus known to his children and a tight-knit circle of readers, was something else altogether. Rather than setting out to defend the orthodox faith, Reimarus, in these so-called *Fragments*, set out to debunk Christianity.

According to Reimarus, Jesus was no religious figure but a Jewish revolutionary. He never performed any miracles, he never preached an otherworldly kingdom of God, and he certainly never rose from the dead. All these notions were to be chalked up to the apostles, not to Jesus himself, who, although beginning with the thought that he was God's agent of political redemption, died in disillusionment. We may have in the Gospels some of the isolated words and actions of Jesus, but these have been dramatically remixed in order to promote the apostolic agenda. Between the historical Jesus and the early church, so Reimarus thought, there was a vast difference, a vast discontinuity. You don't have to be a rocket scientist or a professional theologian to see what is at stake in this claim. If Reimarus was right, Jesus of Nazareth was not the same figure whom the apostles and the early church made him out to be. Christendom has been fooled, and fooled very badly.

Although modern scholars do not give Reimarus much time today (the specifics of his many theories have been largely rejected), his influence on biblical studies was to be huge. One of the important fallouts was a change in the way scholars looked at the Gospels. Certainly, at least since the Renaissance, Bible readers well realized that there was a historical distance between themselves and the events of the first century. The same readers also knew that this historical distance raised problems in understanding: How do we know what the Greek really means? How do we know we have the reading of the original manuscripts? But Reimarus's legacy lay in his introducing a deeply suspicious stance into the modern reading of the Gospels; to modern criticism he bequeathed the assumption that the Gospels depicted a reinvented Jesus rather than Jesus as he really was. By accepting the notion that the first Christians were more interested in presenting Jesus as they needed him to be—teacher, settler of disputes, healer, Lord—than in presenting him truthfully, New Testament scholars suddenly found themselves confronted with the task of discerning what Jesus really said and did. From that point on, when it came to getting back to the words and deeds of the historical Jesus, it was no longer possible to accept the gospel records at face value.

Reimarus understood this perfectly, and indeed, this was his point all along. If Christianity was built on the foundation of historical facts as they were handed down by the apostles, and if it was possible to cast doubt on the apostles' interpretation of those purported facts, then Christianity could be demolished. Rather than being founded on a solid rock, the church was, in Reimarus's view, much more like a house on rickety wooden stilts. Thanks to Reimarus's inspection of the bottom floor, it was now clear to all that even the stilts were, in fact, infested with termites. Without a leg to stand on, Christianity stood condemned.

Not surprisingly, more than a few readers vehemently disagreed with Reimarus's thesis; others were delighted. But one G. E. Lessing (1729–81), the editor of the *Fragments*, who claimed to have found them in the Wolfenbüttel library (when he well knew that he simply borrowed them from Reimarus's daughter, Elize), simultaneously found himself in a state of disagreement and delight. If Reimarus represents the first ring in our circus, Lessing represents the second ring. He disagreed with Reimarus because he was convinced that Christianity did not and could not depend on history. There was a "broad, ugly ditch" between what we can know for certain today and all the uncertainties of ages past. History may contain the story of the apostles' intimation of the truth, but history itself could never vouch for the truth. The accidental truths of history, virtually impossible to verify, could never serve as a secure basis for settling questions such as "Who is God?" and "Who are we?" and "What purpose do we have?" Lessing was pleased with Reimarus not because the author of the *Fragments* disproved Christianity but because he showed why Christianity cannot be tied to history. History was too unstable. Who knows what Jesus was really like? Who knows what words the original manuscripts really contained? As Nietzsche would later put it, history, that is, "the accumulated treasure of the entire past," is but "a host of errors and fantasies."[1] Were Lessing to live long enough to take communion on the crusts of Nietzsche's skepticism, he would not have agreed more.

So for Lessing, it was impossible to verify whether or not the apostles correctly understood and reproduced the words and actions of Jesus. And more importantly, it was beside the point. The record of the Gospels was the apostles' quasi-poetic way of getting at and describing the truth, but it had little to do with whether or not Jesus actually delivered the Sermon on the Mount, and it certainly did not impinge on the possibility of an empty tomb on Easter morning. This meant that while we may have access to interpretations of history, we do not have access to the brute facts of history itself. Because the apostles were only one set of interpreters among many other religious teachers along the course of history, we have no right to grant them special authority. In fact, they did not even claim any special authority. From this Lessing infers that it would be a misuse of the Bible to see it as an oracle or an authoritative source for speaking to modern-day problems.

Enter the representative head of the third ring of our circus: J. M. Goeze. Goeze (1717–86) was an orthodox Lutheran pastor in Hamburg who read Reimarus's *Fragments*, knew full well that Lessing had published them out of more than antiquarian interests, and decided to enter the fray. In a series of letters to the Hamburg newspaper, he explained why he thought Lessing and Reimarus were wrong. According to Goeze, Reimarus was wrong to say that Jesus' goals and intentions were radically different from what the early church envisaged, and Lessing was wrong to say that history was immaterial to Christian faith. So, despite the fact that Goeze was scandalized by Reimarus's claims that Christianity was an invention of the apostles and came into existence through their willful intention to deceive the masses, he was in an important sense much more closely allied to Reimarus than to Lessing. At least, Reimarus and Goeze, had they had the chance to talk it out over a stein of beer, would have agreed that the historical veracity of the Gospels *does* matter, that the past is accessible, and that Christian faith stands or falls on whether the apostles got Jesus right.

Reimarus, Lessing, and Goeze may be taken as the progenitors of three basic approaches to Jesus, for they epitomize how modern-day Christian believers and doubters make sense of the Gospels. For Reimarus, Christianity depended on the accurate transmission of the story of Jesus. Since the Jesus story was consciously distorted, Christianity itself must be a hoax. For modern-day Remarians, if they can prove that Jesus did not actually say or do the things ascribed to him, they can rest satisfied that they have driven a sturdy nail in the coffin of Christianity. Christianity becomes unsustainable because something important has been lost in transmission.

Lessing, too, has his heirs today. Many professing Christians are convinced that the apostles did a rather poor job of conveying the historical Jesus and could not have done so even if they tried. The difficulties of reconstructing what Jesus really said and the original text of scriptures conspire to blunt the sharp claims of

Scripture. It's not that we don't know what Jesus said and didn't say; we just can't be certain. "Besides, why set up the Bible as a false idol?" modern Lessingites might say. "The apostles had their experience of the divine spirit, and now we can have ours, with or without the concrete revelation of Jesus Christ."

Naturally, in speaking to the theological motives behind the history of modern-day Lessings and Reimaruses, it also must be admitted that those who follow in the footsteps of the orthodox Goeze have an equally deep theological stake in how they think about the handed-down story of Jesus. So what about modern-day followers of Goeze? What about those who are convinced that Jesus' words have been faithfully preserved in the Gospels? What drives them? You may call it a compulsive need for everything to be black and white, or you may call it willful blindness. While, as I have already hinted, there is at times some truth to this charge, for now I wish only to make clear that among millions of Christians there is a deep desire to believe that Jesus' words have been faithfully, even if not exhaustively, preserved. So, just as there are some who desperately want Jesus' words to be declared invalid or inauthentic, others are equally keen to see the Gospels as giving an accurate record. Their divergent historical conclusions regarding the Jesus tradition may not follow in lockstep with their theological convictions, but it would be extremely naïve to suppose that our theology (the way we think about God) has no influence on the way we think about Jesus and his words. Our theology may not strictly determine the results of our history ahead of time, but it certainly nudges us.

For this reason, it is only either a spectacular lack of self-awareness or a deep dishonesty that could induce a present-day writer to claim to give an objective or purely historical account of the words of Jesus. I am claiming neither. But I do claim that for historical reasons we can have a great deal of confidence in the scriptural record of Jesus' words—and for that matter, his deeds as well. My own confidence may initially be born of biblical faith, but it is not a faith willfully oblivious to historical realities. Nor is biblical faith to be afraid of historical inquiry; rather, it seeks out such inquiry. If faith and history collide, it might make a pretty mess for a time. But the only worse mess is a stillborn faith that insists on fleeing history and, ultimately, the world in which we live. Never let it be said that the self-revelation of Jesus Christ demands blind acquiescence. Rather, it demands we ask questions when we've come to realize, once again, that we don't yet fully understand the implications of that revelation.

How did Jesus' words safely make it from his mouth to our ears? It is a long journey indeed and, we imagine, one fraught with all kinds of twists, turns, and contingencies. And so we must be up front: because there is so much we don't know, to recount this journey necessarily involves some degree of educated guesswork. But educated guesswork and the forming of hypotheses are not the same as speculation. Nor do such activities necessarily lead us to a kind of nihilistic agnosticism that throws up its hands and says, "Well, who's to know? One theory is as good as another." To go that route, as Lessing, Nietzsche, and Ehrman want to do, is simply to misunderstand the nature of evidence and hypothesizing.

We all form hypotheses constantly on a day-to-day basis, but typically we don't lose sleep wondering whether we can be 100 percent certain about our hypotheses. When I drink a cup of tea at night before bed, I may lie awake from the caffeine, but I don't lie awake wondering whether my wife has poisoned it. I suppose there is always a theoretical possibility that she has. But even if that possibility exists, because it is such a slim probability (although ever so slightly weightier, I suppose, on the days I deserve to have my tea poisoned), my working hypothesis that I will be waking up the next morning remains firm. As long as she is the one making the tea, I cannot attain certainty. I must be content with hypothesis. But in practical terms, the difference between a very strong hypothesis and certainty (whatever that is—after all, how can I be so sure that there wasn't tampering at the factory, warehouses, or retailer?) is often negligible.

It seems to me that Lessing's error lay in his demand that in order for Goeze and the orthodox Christians to be right, they must validate their faith by appealing to *indisputable* certainties. Of course, had you accompanied Herr Lessing on his everyday business, I'm sure you would have found him being inconsistent with his own rule: no one goes through life committing himself or herself only on the basis of what is absolutely certain, Lessing's "necessary truths of reason." Life regularly demands commitments from us, and almost nothing in life is certain in the way that Lessing seems to define certainty. Why Lessing requires a degree of certainty for metaphysical decisions (How do I know who God is? How do I know what God wants from me?) that is of a completely higher and different order than what sane people require for everyday decisions (Should I drink this tea offered me? How do I know it's not poisoned?) escapes me. That the Bible appeals to the evidentiary, that "which we have seen with our eyes, which we have looked upon, and our hands have handled" (1 John 1:1), requires that we confirm the claims of Scripture very much like we confirm truth claims in all other areas of life. Unwillingness to do so means we have failed to take the Bible and the incarnation itself on their own terms.

Of course we can pursue the alternative and forget all about this business of history, evidence, and hypothesis. We can simply go back to pretending—as has too often been the mental instinct of too many conservative Christians—that the Bible and the words of Jesus just dropped out of heaven into our laps. We have the option of going back, in other words, to a situation in which we cease to think as historians. But even if we can live for a while with this inner inconsistency between our steadfast theology and our murky history, eventually the tension becomes unbearable. Our intellectual sin will find us out—perhaps in an unexpected moment of doubt, perhaps through a conversation with a stranger, or perhaps through our children as they grow older and begin to grapple aloud with issues of faith and history. Unless we satisfy ourselves that the words of Jesus have some historical legitimization, we are like Steve Martin's *Man with Two Brains*, living dualistically in two separate worlds. God's becoming flesh demands that the world of faith and the workaday world of time, space, and history be one and the same.

I believe that conservative Christianity's tendency to succumb to this kind of dualism has to do with its having been duped by the same philosophical framework that served Lessing so well. Somehow many of us have gotten it into our minds—thanks in no small part to Enlightenment thinkers like René Descartes and Francis Bacon—that truth must be a risk-free venture, leaving us with only two options: absolute certainty or thoroughgoing skepticism. But that is not what Scripture says. Scripture says that faith "is the substance of things hoped for, the evidence of things not seen" (Heb. 11:1). This certainty proceeds from the assurance that God has revealed himself; it is not an absolute certainty, but it is a certainty that was sufficient to compel the heroes of the faith to do amazing and courageous deeds. It is this faith, not the mental gymnastics of unimpeachable certainty, for which the ancients were commended.

Of course, if God were to deliver his self-revelation by dropping it directly from heaven, that would greatly reduce risk and assuage any fear that parts of it were indeed garbled in transmission. (Of course, this would not circumvent the problem as to how we know that the book deposit really came from heaven.) But this would not be Christianity. For, again, the center of Christianity is the incarnation. From the beginning we know that God was not averse to entrusting revelation to an unfolding process of transmission—and a *human* process at that.

That remains the scandal. Second-century Gnostics could not believe that God would entrust himself to the vagaries of flesh; modern-day Islam is no less incredulous in regard to the claim. But God saw fit to reveal himself as Word in flesh. God spoke decisively and once and for all in the Son (Heb. 1:2), with the Son, at least as far as our apprehension of him was concerned, also "having *become* so much better than the angels" (Heb. 1:4, emphasis mine). Christ is the truth; he does not become the truth. But there is a sense in which truth is progressively revealed to us, even as we go about reconstructing the original text of the New Testament, even as we examine history.

But history can be messy; history leaves room for error. Since God saw fit to continue to use flesh (this time sinful flesh) in

45

passing down the sum and substance of that Word through a process of transmission, this unavoidably leaves open the possibility that some of Jesus' words *were* lost in transmission. Perhaps many of us would prefer for God not to have taken this sort of risk. But if God was not averse to risk when he gave the babe in the manger in the days of Herod and high infant mortality rates, why should we expect him to manage matters any differently when it comes to giving the Word? Like the Son himself, the transmitted revelation about the Son is a gift that has been delivered once for all, and its meaning is sufficiently clear to all who would seek to respond to it. Even so, again like our understanding of the Son, our understanding of Scripture, its message and its precise contents, is a work in progress. For Lessing and his heirs, the inability of Goeze to stake a more certain claim, an absolute claim, undermines the Christian case completely.

For Christians, the paradoxical notion that Christ is an absolute given, yet one that is being slowly unpacked in our collective understanding, allows for a properly nuanced theory of knowledge (epistemology). It's ironic that orthodox Christians are often accused of constructing a reality that is all too black and white, all too neat and tidy, when actually, it is Lessing and Ehrman who demand that certainty be an all-or-nothing deal. Traditional Christianity has never construed truth that way, for truth came in a person. And a person can be untidy.

When we imagine the earliest Christian martyrs—back in the days before anyone wondered about the ethics of handing the Christians over to the lions—standing on the floor of the arena of the Circus Maximus, we have to suppose that at least some thought about getting out of their predicament by renouncing their Christian faith. But history tells us that they remained stead-fast. What were they thinking? Did anyone think to himself or herself, *You know, I've become a Christian, but I never really took the time to verify my faith with 100 percent certainty. Maybe I should recant, take my leave and do the appropriate research and analysis that will leave absolutely no doubt as to the validity of my claims.* I don't think so. The faith of the early Christians was not a blind faith. Rather, it seems to have been a faith that took history (the story of Jesus) seriously but also knew the limits of reconstructing that story and its transmission. Our inability to reconstruct that story and its transmission with watertight certainty should not tempt us to become historically blind. On the contrary, we should embrace history not only because it has the promise of illuminating the plausibility of Christian belief, but also because history is an important midwife in the long, arduous, and mystery-laden deliv-ery of truth. Researching history is worth the risk and, in fact, is demanded by the incarnation itself. And if it should land us only short of perfect certainty, it only means that we are not God.

FOUR

LORD OF
THE RING

I continue to appreciate the Bible and the many and varied
messages it contains—much as I have come to appreciate
the other writings of early Christians from about the same
time and soon thereafter, the writings of lesser-known
figures such as Ignatius of Antioch, Clement of Rome, and
Barnabas of Alexandria, and much as I have come to
appreciate the writings of persons of other faiths at
roughly the same time, the writings of Josephus, and
Lucian of Samosata, and Plutarch.

—BART EHRMAN, *Misquoting Jesus*

It was January of my senior year, and I was continuing in my personal study of the Bible. By this time, in order to speed things along, I had bought an English version. I was still trying to figure out what the Bible was really saying, or at least what it might say to me, and I believed all along that somehow I could possibly make sense of it all. With this hope in mind, I had signed up for a course in comparative religions, taught by the school chaplain, Mr. McIlhiney. (He was actually ordained and had an earned doctorate but had the good pastoral sense to have us call him "*Mr. McIlhiney*.") The major textbook for the course was Huston Smith's *The Religions of Man*.[1] As was typical of courses taught at Exeter, our seats were arranged in a ring.

Unfortunately, in this case, the face-to-face format did little to spur conversation as we muddled our way through the major faiths. Throughout the course, Mr. McIlhiney tried his best to get the conversation rolling by asking appropriately open-ended questions. But time and again these prompts would be followed by excruciatingly long, uncomfortable pauses. I think we all would have liked the class to flow better, at least for our instructor's sake.

He was—and I'm sure still is—the nicest guy you could meet, and you didn't want to let him down if you could help it. But reading or no reading, I think we felt in over our heads. And the more we talked, the more we began to realize that we were merely pooling our ignorance on these matters. It was like Howie Long hosting an NFL post-game analysis only to discover that he had convened a panel of individuals who thought that a blitz was one of Santa's reindeer. And of course it fell to poor Mr. McIlhiney to smile and affirm our often ludicrous opinions, engage us on matters that were quite foreign to most of us, and, finally, participation failing, make pronouncements of his own before our little circle. He had de facto acquired the unenviable job of being lord of the ring.

But for me there was also something off-putting, maybe even intuitively profane, about the process. Who were we, I was beginning to think, that we, a small class of Ivy League–bound preppies, had the right to sit around and evaluate what the world believed about this and that? A few years prior, I wouldn't have been bothered in the least. Were it my sophomore year in high school, I would have been glad to opine ignorantly on the relative merits of the world religions, as anyone would compare the quality of their favorite Mexican, Chinese, and Italian restaurants. But apparently something was beginning to happen in the way I was thinking about religion. I was beginning to feel that our class's commitment to religious noncommitment, rather than being a boon to our objective analysis, was actually a hindrance.

I don't blame Mr. McIlhiney. This was the course he was assigned to teach, and teach it this way he must. But there is a certain oddity in carrying on conversations about Islam, Christianity, and the rest as if their bottom line didn't matter. If there was a bottom line at all, it was that the bottom line of these religions *cannot* matter. The effect is stultifying.

On reflection, this also strikes me as mildly bizarre. Consider, for example, if FOX Sports ran its autumn Sunday afternoon broadcasts the way most learning institutions carry out their religious instruction. It would mean that John Madden not only should withhold his opinion as to whom he wants to win the Super Bowl (fair enough) but also should not, as a matter of principle, even care. It has long been felt that it is in the best interests of Western society, as well as the state that seeks at all costs to keep that society cohesive, that those who serve as commentators for the World Religions Playoffs can be qualified as long as they do not personally involve themselves in the outcome of the game. This creates a situation in which those who teach religion and write books on it have a vested professional interest in remaining aloof from and suspicious of the claims that those same religions make.

In his own time, Nietzsche predicted that the state would come to control education and that, when it did, meaningful cultural and individual expression would die. This is because the state demands that all subversive and destabilizing thought systems, such as, I suppose, the belief that Jesus was bodily and uniquely raised from the dead, be domesticated and brought into submission. On this score, I think, Nietzsche has been proven right. The top-down enforcement of tolerance is no bad thing so long as the principle of tolerance applies to the *way* we discuss life's important questions. But when the principle of tolerance goes beyond this so as to require that we answer life's important questions with a certain prescribed solution, then tolerance itself becomes God and all the other candidates (Jesus Christ, Allah, Yahweh, etc.) are relegated to playing backup quarterback.

This brings us back to the quotation that heads up this chapter. On one level, the appreciative sentiments concerning the New Testament authors, Ignatius of Antioch, Josephus the Jew, and Plutarch the Greek reflect a generous spirit—a point that itself is to be appreciated. However, when one hears such even-handed approval for such a diverse cast of thinkers who believe contradictory things, one may be forgiven for suspecting that something is afoot. It seems that this judgment, rather than arising out of a personal wrestling with their claims, is simply the rehearsing of a script beholden to Lessing's vision and the conformist project of the Western state. Some people consider agnosticism a radical position. This is a mistake. Playing right into the hands of the conformist state and implying nothing that is not the quintessence of social acceptability, agnosticism is about as socially-politically conservative as you can get. Christian orthodoxy, on the other hand, is deeply subversive. It is subversive not because it is uncivil (on the contrary, civility is part and parcel of the Christian call) but because it stoutly refuses to be cowed by any agenda, state sponsored or otherwise, that competes with the agenda of Jesus' kingdom.

Not that I could have put all this together as a seventeen-year-old sitting in Mr. McIlhiney's class, but nonetheless I felt vaguely inwardly resistant for *some* reason. I allowed myself to be distracted. I can remember looking down into the carpet. I remember being mesmerized by the sight of my instructor's very long legs twirling themselves like a vine around each other and the leg of his chair. How did he do that anyway? All the while, I can't remember anyone raising the question as to why we were so attached to being detached.

And so Mr. Mac (as we fondly called him) would have a tough time with a very tough bunch. But on the first day of the course, things were different. At least for the first class everyone's hopes spring eternal. At the end of that class, he reminded us of our night's assignment, the chapter on Hinduism. "Once you read this chapter," he said cheerily, "it will make partial converts out of you all."

Excellent, I thought to myself. Maybe this was my ticket. I unconsciously felt as if I needed *something*, perhaps something like Hinduism, to counter the uncomfortably stark words of Jesus. Jesus, I was continuing to find, was not one to mince words. "But whoever slaps you on your right cheek, turn the other to him also" (Matt. 5:39). "If your right eye causes you to sin, pluck it out and cast it from you" (Matt. 5:29). "If anyone desires to come after Me, let him deny himself, and take up his cross daily, and follow Me" (Luke 9:23). I was at once repelled and attracted by these words. My ambivalence about Jesus was only growing stronger. On the one hand, his teachings seemed to ring beautiful and true, but on the other hand, I was not ready to let his words have their way with me. I was on the lookout for a better offer.

I couldn't wait to start reading about Hinduism. And so I went back to my dorm room and read. Later that day when it was time to go to wrestling practice, I took my copy of Huston Smith with me and read, with nose firmly planted in book, as I walked the short distance from Wentworth Hall to the gym. Looking up to make sure I was not about to trip on the snow or something else, I saw Mr. McIlhiney walking on the path toward me. It suddenly occurred to me that this was a serendipitous opportunity to play the suck-up. "Hey, look what I'm reading," I said, half kidding but also half earnest in the hope that he would somehow reward my being so enthralled with the subject matter that I could not even put the book down while walking about campus. I thought I had scored at least a few brownie points.

Perhaps I had. But they were not to last long. I can't remember what I ended up getting in that class, but I do remember it was one of the lowest grades I received at Exeter. In retrospect, this is somewhat amazing because not only had I read and thoroughly digested the chapter on Hinduism, but I had done the same with the chapter on Buddhism. In fact, I was so taken with the chapter on Buddhism, I set myself to practicing Zen Buddhism. A Zen master from Boston, whom Mr. McIlhiney had introduced to the class, got me started. I had learned to practice full lotus position up to an hour a day. If anyone had done extra credit, it would have been me. But my grade certainly didn't reflect it. Maybe I should have participated more.

It was during that course that our chaplain also introduced us to the famous metaphor of the elephant. How do we explain the differences in world religions and their competing truth claims? One explanation Mr. McIlhiney shared goes something like this. Humanity's search for God is like a collection of blind men feeling their way along an elephant. Some feel the toenails and say, "The elephant is like this." Others feel the long, hairy trunk and say, "The elephant is like this." Still others feel the tail and others feel the tusk. They all experience one and the same elephant but in different ways.

For the time being, this seemed like an entirely satisfactory way of tying it all together. Christians are like the folks at the tusk—all those hard sayings. Others, maybe the Jews, feel the ear. I'm not sure whom we would assign to the tail. But in the end, it's all the same God, and we all have our equally legitimate paths to getting to this God. Christian, Hindu, Buddhist, Jew, Muslim. Working to the best of our ability, all of us are reaping equally limited rewards, and all of us are blind as a bat all the while (well, almost all of us).

What a welcome relief that metaphor was to someone struggling with Jesus and his words. You see, if humanity really is like a bunch of blind elephant–gropers, then that means that Jesus Christ is only part of the elephant and not the elephant itself. This way of looking at things certainly puts Jesus, as it were, in his place. Moreover, when it comes to Jesus' talking of heaven and hell (which, I came to find, he did a lot), the elephant metaphor is of immense help. When the blind man feels the point of the tusk, he thinks, *This must be hell.* When the blind woman feels its smoothness, she thinks, *Ah, heaven.* Heaven and hell then were only ways of talking about the experience of God, but they didn't refer to any objective reality outside of themselves. With his vision of the world with no heaven above and no hell below, John Lennon could not have been more pleased. I could not have been more pleased either.

Equally happy would have been our friend Gotthold Lessing. Much of what drove Lessing's theological agenda was his insistence that the scourge of peaceful societal existence was certain people's insistence that they and they alone had the truth. This comes out in his parable of the three rings, found in his play *Nathan the Wise.* According to this story, it was the practice of a particular ancient Eastern family for the father of the household to bequeath to his son a ring of secret power, the power to be loved by God and others. Unfortunately, there was a problem.

The man had three sons, and he loved all three equally. As a result, he decided to give not one but three rings to his sons—one being the authentic ring and the other two being very good imitations. When the father passed away, each son considered that he alone had the right ring. When they brought the matter to court, the judge issued this verdict:

> But my advice is this:
> You take the matter as it stands,
> If each one had his ring straight from his father,
> So let each believe his ring the true one.
> 'Tis possible your father would not longer tolerate
> The tyranny of this one ring in his family,
> And surely loved you all—and all alike,
> And that he would not two oppress
> By favoring the third.[2]

Elsewhere in the play it becomes obvious that this is a very thinly veiled parable about religion. Apparently for Lessing, if you favor one religious option, this constitutes oppression. In order to avoid this unfortunate tyranny, it is best to assume that at least for the duration of earthly existence there is no way of knowing who has the right ring. In essence Lessing calls for a "No Religion Left Behind" policy, a mandated, outcome-based education of humankind. Whatever else happens, no one fails; everyone gets it right because, paradoxically, everyone has gotten it wrong—more exactly, everyone has gotten it wrong except for the one mandating the policy.

While it appears that both the elephant metaphor and the idea behind Lessing's parable of three rings were humble attempts to get everyone to respect one another's position, it did not occur to me at the time that through such approaches we were, in fact, only arrogating to ourselves a superior vantage point and simultaneously digging ourselves into a deeper hole of religious supremacy. The one who explains the diversity of world religions by appealing to the well-worn metaphor of the elephant is actually implicitly saying, "While certain blind folk are groping their way around the isolated parts of the elephant of God, I and those who think like me are the only ones who have stepped back and have seen the whole elephant. We alone are privileged to know that all these different religions are simply part of this one greater whole." It is tantamount to saying, "We alone have seen all of God." Lessing's parable of the three rings is likewise no less hubristic, no less condescending. In claiming to have the final word on the relative claims of the plaintiff brothers, Lessing is, in fact, positioning himself as the judge and the lord of the ring.

If the exclusive nature of the truth claims of the Abrahamic faiths (Christianity, Islam, and Judaism) is offensive to the Lessings of today, including Lennon and apparently Ehrman as well, this offense, I believe, pales in comparison with those who in so many ways pat each of three sons on the head and say, "Now, you three brothers, stop fighting about whose imaginary friend is better, but run along now and play." While the three Abrahamic faiths may have serious mutual disagreement among themselves, at least they are in a position to take one another's claims seriously and contest them on a level playing field. But post-Enlightenment, Western liberalism, in all its various religious and nonreligious guises, claims a superior vantage point and fails to take them seriously altogether.

Thus, Lessing bequeaths to his children only a faux tolerance, for it is a tolerance that demands the removal of any god who reveals himself in a particular way to a particular people. His project is no less tyrannical and no less totalizing than any other of the major offers sitting on the table long before he was born. In this respect the Enlightenment project is deeply exclusive. According to its logic, only those who agree with this way of seeing things are "enlightened," while presumably those who hold out the possibility that a particular god can been revealed in the particulars of history are "unenlightened," that is, in the dark.

Over time I would come to realize how, simply by growing up in the West, I was subject to that project. Once I realized this, I then realized that Jesus' announcement of the kingdom of heaven did not mean I would have to *start* living in subservience to a kingdom. The truth was that, whatever my delusions of personal freedom, I was already by default living in a kingdom and in subjection to its ideals. Jesus' call to the individual involves not the forfeiting of freedom but rather the acquiescence to the proposition that his kingdom is superior to the kingdom to which the individual is already indentured.

The reason I rehearse these issues at length is that when it comes to the words of Jesus, there is among scholars a deeply ingrained pressure toward historical agnosticism (we can't know what Jesus really said). This is no innocent posture, for this historical agnosticism is in large part driven by a culture-wide religious agnosticism (we can't know if Jesus' words are true). Historical agnosticism and religious agnosticism: they feed off of each other. Here's why. If we can know what Jesus said, that puts us in a position whereby we must decide on Jesus. Either he was who he and his followers claimed him to be, or he was not. But if we cannot get back to Jesus because his words and very identity have been all but lost in transmission, then this keeps alive a corresponding agnosticism when it comes to weighing Jesus' claims against other counteroffers.

But there is a second reason for this discussion of the problem of religious diversity: how we handle religious diversity comes to bear on our modern study of Jesus' words. For when we behold the myriad of contemporary visions as to who Jesus was, we see beneath the diversity that there are in fact two main ways of looking at Jesus: one that fits hand in glove with the ideals of the Enlightenment, and one that does not. The first stream of interpretation tends to emphasize Jesus as a moral sage whose observations are of a very general nature and whose message is not related to the Judaism of his day. On this view, if Jesus wanted to say anything at all to Judaism, it was only that he was unhappy with their old way of doing things and their legalistic externalism. This Jesus, far from being an eschatological agent of God, was simply an extraordinarily insightful person whose message can be conveniently subsumed within this heavenless, religionless brotherhood of man. For those who want their Jesus but want to bring him in line with the constraints of post-Enlightenment Western liberalism, the first stream of interpretation is very attractive.

The other broad line of interpretation, by contrast, takes Jesus' Jewishness very seriously. If Jesus was a first-century Jew, and this background becomes the primary means by which we understand his ministry and message, then we will also likely conclude two things: first, that Jesus believed in election (that God reveals himself in special ways to some people and not others), and second, that he expected God to work decisively and uniquely through Israel, and by extension himself, in order to achieve a particular goal. On this view, we cannot ignore that much of Jesus' message was geared not just to a Jewish audience but to a Jewish audience *as Jews*; on this view, too, Jesus expected God to break into history, during his time, in a special way.

But how do such strong claims square with the notion, which post-Enlightenment liberalism wants to believe, that we all at least in theory have the bequeathed ring or that we are all blindly feeling our way around the elephant? Unfortunately, not very well. For if Jesus really did believe that salvation was from the Jews and that the God of Israel was doing something unprecedented and unrepeatable in him, then it is at this point that Jesus and Western modernity come to an irresolvable impasse. One of the two will have to step aside. Either Jesus was deluded in his hope and must say, "Excuse me, I was wrong about having the backing of the God of Israel," or Jesus has the right of way. If the former is the case, as Reimarus sought to prove, then we must deal with Jesus as we would a crank at a concert who has rushed the stage and hijacked the microphone. But if the latter is the case, then we quickly realize that no amount of transposing will bring Jesus into tune with Western culture's ongoing performance of "Imagine." (A much better-fitting song would be the apocalyptic strains of the Doors' "The End.") In the case of the Jewish Jesus, we must either treat him as a historical curiosity who must ultimately be escorted off the stage or give him a stage of his own and allow him to challenge our regnant North American idols. But this is the point: it is hard, if not impossible, to take Jesus' Judaism seriously and make him into a poster child for Western liberalism.[3]

As the fellowship of Jesus scholars takes up its quest of the prized ring, the historical Jesus himself, I think that there are some reconstructions that make sense and some that don't. In the following chapter, I shall argue that the paradigm that makes the best sense of the data is the paradigm that takes Jesus seriously as a Jew and, more than that, as one who nurtured a vision for Israel. Once this point is established, we will be ready to speak specifically, in chapter six, to Jesus' words. In my view, if you forgo laying this foundation, the question of Jesus' historical identity, you may be forced to agree with the diagnosis that Jesus' words were likely lost in transmission. If you are interested in a second opinion, read on.

FIVE

JESUS THE JEW

Christianity began, of course, with Jesus, who was himself a Jewish rabbi (teacher) who accepted the authority of the Torah, and possibly other sacred Jewish books, and taught his interpretation of those books to his disciples. Like other rabbis of his day, Jesus maintained that God's will could be found in the sacred texts, especially the Law of Moses. He read these scriptures, studied these scriptures, interpreted these scriptures, adhered to these scriptures, and taught these scriptures.

—BART EHRMAN, *Misquoting Jesus*

My roommate at boarding school was not what you would call a particularly religious person. He was extremely likable, but he had none of the characteristics you would typically associate with "religious people." Like the rest of us high school seniors, he had sex on the brain (and was not any slower than the rest of us in telling you exactly what his brain was thinking at any given moment). Like many of us, including myself, he was not averse to underage and, therefore, underhanded procurement of alcoholic beverages. And like many of us (honestly, I can't remember how true this was of me), he swore a blue streak. But he was raised in a Roman Catholic home and would show his Catholic colors every now and again.

In the spring of 1982, my roommate decided that he wanted to attend mass during Holy Week, the week leading up to Easter. By this time I had pretty much read everything the New Testament had to say about the life of Jesus and decided that, if he didn't mind, I would go along. I came to find that Catholics did a lot of church the week before Easter. First, there was this thing called "*Monday* [*sic*] Thursday," which had something to do with Jesus washing his disciples' feet. Our trip to Saint Mike's, as the church was affectionately called, was a new experience for me. It was, of course, not nearly as new and strange for "my favorite roommate" (I called him that a lot). The next evening was to be the Good Friday service, the commemoration of Jesus' crucifixion. If I had found Thursday night's service long, Roomie assured me, Friday's service would be much longer. Actually, I hadn't found Thursday's service too long; neither had he. And so we both decided to go back.

On the evening of Good Friday, after grabbing a bite at the dining hall, we walked down the street to St. Michael's once again. This time the pews were much more crowded. We slipped in and took our places toward the back. He gave me some orientation as to what was about to transpire, including the celebration of the Eucharist, or what Protestants call the Lord's Supper. From that point on we didn't speak to each other again until the end of the service, which was to be some two hours later. I remember relishing the fact that it was going to be a long service. This gave me some more time to put my thoughts together about what all of this meant.

As the service began, I did my best to speak when expected to speak, to stay quiet when expected to stay quiet, and to kneel when expected to kneel. Sometimes for those worshipping in new environments, there is a terrible self-consciousness about these things. But when you're seventeen, just as one of the chief curses is an extreme self-consciousness in regard to matters that no one but God even notices, so too, paradoxically, one of the chief blessings is a brusque uninhibitedness in situations where people do well to forget themselves.

In the midst of it all, my eyes kept fastening themselves on the sculpted wooden figure hanging on the cross behind the altar. *All this*, I thought to myself, *all the churches, all the people in the churches, all their beliefs and ways of going about things—all this rides on Jesus.* Who do people say that this Jesus was? What was it these Christians believed about Jesus? And were they right? I kept focusing on the serene yet haggard face looking down from the cross, as if looking at Jesus might bring me closer to the truth. The face only indirectly stared back, as if to say, "And, you, who do you say that I am?" I wondered.

In some sense, I still wonder today. But the questions I have now are of a very different sort than the ones I was asking when I was sitting in that pew twenty-five years ago. There was, I felt, no one at hand who could really answer my questions. But even if there was someone around, where would that person begin? Where would *I*, given where I stand today, begin? What might I say if it were possible for me-now to communicate with me-then? There would no doubt be a lot I could and would say about the theological significance of Jesus—why he came, what he said about himself, why he demands a response—these issues are of first significance.

But another set of issues was beginning to plague me more at that time, and these issues related to the historical Jesus. It's no bad thing when talking about Jesus to start with his theological significance. It is a bad thing, however, to pretend that Jesus' theological significance precludes our taking seriously historical issues. I have already discussed this at length.

So what about Jesus and what about his words? What might a historian say? In the next chapter, I will discuss the historical value of the sources on Jesus and the degree to which we can trust their authenticity. But as a prelude to that discussion, it needs to be pointed out once again that when Jesus historians come to certain conclusions about Jesus, the conclusions almost always entail certain assumptions made ahead of time. In other words, Jesus scholars undertake their quest for Jesus using methods that presuppose that the elusive Palestinian has in some sense already been found. If this sounds somewhat circular, it probably means you're following what I am saying. But it is not necessarily a vicious circularity; it does not necessarily involve, in other words, the logical fallacy of question begging.

Toward explaining why, let me get right to some basic assumptions, that is, what scholars typically believe about Jesus before they work out the facts about Jesus. There are many ways to lay this out, but I believe two questions are critical. The first is this: is Jesus to be understood within a primarily Hellenistic context or within a more thoroughgoing Jewish context? In answering this, we must think along the lines of a spectrum. Anybody and everybody who lived in the first-century world absorbed into their lifeblood the Greek ethos of Alexander the Great's now-defunct empire. To live when Jesus lived meant to live and breathe in the culture of the Greeks. At the same time, Jesus was Jewish. Even if nineteenth-century scholar Ernst Renan preferred to think that "Jesus ceased to be a Jew," the truth cannot be anywhere near this. There are far too many indications of Jesus' Jewishness to think that he ever left his Jewish heritage entirely behind. But to what extent was Jesus influenced by the thoughtway of Graeco-Roman culture? Conversely, how Jewish was Jesus? That's the first question.

The second question is this: did Jesus have any sense of being the founder of a movement that would survive beyond him? Were Jesus' followers along for a short ride, or was there something institutional and programmatic about the early Jesus movement?

Another way of putting this question is to ask whether Jesus or his disciples had a vision that would eventually demand some kind of long-term organizational or political structure.

The two questions—"Was Jesus a Hellenist or a Jew?" and "Was Jesus a movement founder?"—are related. Here's why. Let's assume for the moment that Jesus was deeply steeped in Hellenistic culture and that the closest analogy to Jesus is the itinerant Cynic philosopher. Traveling philosophers were actually fairly common sights in the first-century world, and it is not a priori implausible that Jesus identified himself with this calling. Over the course of antiquity, certain Greek philosophers did, in fact, give rise to movements and schools that continued to exist for centuries after them, and so it is not out of the question that Jesus as a wandering philosopher gathered disciples with a view to perpetuating his teaching. If Jesus was a Hellenist, say, for example, a Cynic philosopher, it is not impossible that he would have also been a movement founder. In this case, we might expect his movement to carry on his teachings, and little more than that, after his death.

But this is not what happened. Rather, after Jesus is crucified and resurrected (let's bracket the question as to what resurrection actually means), his disciples don't seem to be preaching so much what Jesus preached but rather preaching Jesus himself. This is not the kind of thing we expect from the followers of a Cynic philosopher. That Jesus moved from being "the proclaimer" to "the proclaimed one" may, of course, be the result of a gross misunderstanding on the disciples' part, but then there must be some explanation as to how that misunderstanding took root in the first place. The early Christians firmly held that Jesus was the long-awaited Messiah. This is historically indubitable. If Jesus was merely an itinerant philosopher, how do we get from this status to Messiah? It's a long jump.

Therefore, if you are of the view that Jesus' mental instincts were those of a Hellenist philosopher, the problem you face is not in explaining why Jesus remained popular after his death but in explaining why Jesus was proclaimed as the Messiah after his death. There were numerous philosophers who maintained followings in those days. None of them, as far as we can tell, were regarded as messianic at any point either before or after their deaths. The far easier route is to say that the early church declared Jesus to be Messiah because Jesus, in very Jewish fashion, gave ample, even if largely implicit, indication that he believed himself to be that Messiah. That is why, I believe, most scholars who understand Jesus' background as primarily Hellenistic also typically take the view that Jesus did not intend to found a movement, much less have a movement started in his name. On the face of it, Jesus as an essentially Jewish movement founder makes far better sense than Jesus as a Hellenistic movement founder.

If we consider what even the more skeptical of Jesus scholars regard as indubitable fact, we find that Jesus' role as Jewish movement founder is borne out beautifully. According to most scholars, it is virtually certain that Jesus cleansed the temple (Mark 11:12–18). He also, equally indisputably, reclined with his disciples to take in an evening meal the day before his death (Mark 14:12–26). The two events, happening a few days within each other, are in fact interconnected and mutually interpreting.

This becomes clear on consideration of the significance of what Jesus was doing in cleansing the temple and sharing a final meal with his disciples. Whatever the various motives Jesus may have had when he overturned the tables of the money changers (a complex question in its own right), one thing clearly emerges from the record: that Jesus was declaring the imminent destruction of the temple, which would presumably then be restored anew by God under new leadership. By flipping the tables in the temple, Jesus was essentially saying, "God is going to flip this house—after some pretty serious gutting." This has been argued convincingly by more than a few scholars.[1]

Now, whatever Jesus scholars are willing to say about the substance of the Lord's Supper tradition, one thing stands out in the tradition: that Jesus used bread and wine in a symbolic manner. When Jesus says, "This is My body" (Mark 14:22), it seems that Jesus was denoting a sacrifice, whereby he himself played the role of the sacrificial victim. By that time in Judaism, the notion of a martyr dying an atoning death on behalf of Israel was already well established. And when the atoning death of such martyrs is described, it is not atypical for the language of that description to be temple language (2 Macc. 7). Jesus' actions at the Last Supper indicate that he is self-consciously thinking of himself along the same trajectory.

So the cleansing of the temple and the Last Supper together suggest that in Jesus' mind there was something deeply flawed about the present temple system. This temple was coming to an end (as is made clear in Mark 13), and Jesus himself was somehow taking on the function of the new temple. In this case, Jesus' death would be the inaugural sacrifice for this new temple, which would presumably be constituted around his band of disciples. That is also, by the way, exactly why Jesus chose twelve disciples. The twelve disciples stood for the new and restored twelve tribes of

Israel. In ancient Judaism, the temple represented and embodied the twelve tribes of Israel, just as the twelve tribes represented and embodied the temple (see Exod. 19:6). Jesus' ragtag band of twelve followers were not just followers; they were the building blocks of the new temple.[2]

This line of reasoning does not resolve the goals and precise nature of Jesus' ministry; nor does it bring into immediate focus the import of his teaching. But what it does do is give us a basis for assuming that when Jesus spoke, he spoke a message that was drawn from Scripture and pertained to an audience that would survive Jesus. In a sense, this is to say no more than that Jesus' self-consciousness as an agent of God's purposes had analogy with the way those in John's movement, the Qumran covenanters, and even the Pharisees thought of themselves. To gather a following in first-century Judaism, whose objectives were to achieve the divine destiny of Israel (however it may have been conceived), was no small thing. Individuals who do such things will attract attention and speculation, much as the Jesus movement is reported to have done (Matt. 16:13–14). And if the leader of such a movement were to teach on what God was doing through this movement, we must imagine that his followers would have had more than a casual interest in this teaching. Jesus' role as the publicly recognized leader of a substitute-temple movement has important implications for our understanding of not only the very Jewish nature of his message but also the way his words would come to be preserved.

Despite all this, it has, oddly enough, not been until the past several decades that the Jewishness of Jesus has been taken seriously in Jesus scholarship. There are, I think, reasons it is only now that this idea has come into its own; these reasons have to do with the spirit of the times reaching all the way back to the late eighteenth century. When Reimarus wrote his *Fragments*, his thesis was recognized as scandalous not least because he positioned Jesus squarely within the context of first-century Judaism, at least as Reimarus understood it. A good number of those writing after Reimarus followed the author of the *Fragments* down the path of rationalism, but very few saw any value in understanding Jesus in Jewish terms.

That is because there was a forceful undercurrent in the countless nineteenth-century "lives of Jesus," which was going the reverse direction. For most nineteenth-century writers, Jesus' genius lay in his insistence that it was high time to leave behind what they believed to be a paltry and largely externalistic religion of his Jewish forebearers. In place of Reimarus's Jewish revolutionary figure was a romanticized Jesus, a polite and moral and gentlemanly Jesus, a Jesus every nineteenth-century, European, middle-class, non-Jewish mother would want her son to emulate. This reflects the fact that, as a whole, nineteenth-century Protestant Europe did not think highly of Judaism. Whatever Jesus was, he was not about to be seen as a Jew.

And who knows? Perhaps post-Enlightenment Europe would have lived happily with their portrait of a domesticated, non-Jewish Jesus were it not for the likes of one man, Albert Schweitzer, who blew the whistle on the whole affair. In his breathtaking *The Quest of the Historical Jesus* (1906), Schweitzer looks back on Jesus scholarship from Reimarus up until Schweitzer's own time and, like Toto in *The Wizard of Oz*, runs up to the curtain and pulls on the trouser cuffs of those who, by manipulating the data, had projected a Jesus who was far from the historical reality. According to Schweitzer, Jesus was not at all like he was made out to be in the nineteenth century, which we now call the First Quest of the Historical Jesus. Instead, the true Jesus was a near-raving eschatological prophet who preached the coming Son of Man who would usher in the final age of Israel. Eventually, Jesus came to realize that he himself was the Son of Man, and so he forced the hand of history and the hand of God by casting himself, so to speak, on a Roman cross. Realizing, alas too late, that nothing was coming of it, Schweitzer's Jesus gasps, "My God, my God, why have you forsaken me?" The end.

Unfortunately, Schweitzer's Jesus did not make for a very pretty picture on a number of theological fronts. Homiletically, it's hard to preach a Jesus who basically got it wrong and ended his life as a pathetic, dismal failure. Schweitzer's Jesus was not a man who could fire the contemporary imagination; much less could this Jesus fill the church pews. As a result, at least at the time of its publication, Schweitzer's book was largely ignored. It was as if the collective theological consciousness of Western Europe, the wizard himself, had said, "Pay no attention to that man behind the curtain!" Toto (that is, Schweitzer) was reined in and the lay admirers of Jesus continued to stand in awe of the image of Jesus the philosophical moral genius.

Yet most scholars knew deep down that the gig was up and that Schweitzer was right about how Jesus' image had been engineered. There *was* a man behind the curtain. In its attempt to charm its reading public with no small measure of smoke and mirrors, so much of Jesus scholarship had lost its soul. Pull the right levers and Jesus becomes what you want him to become. For some decades, it took some nerve to utter even a word about Jesus. Looking back, we can see that Schweitzer's book served as a gravestone for the First Quest.

In due course came the Second Quest of the Historical Jesus, and the Second Quest begat the Third Quest. Although the Second Quest (which I will discuss more fully in the next chapter) is far from dead, most scholars writing on Jesus today write within the vein of the Third Quest. The Third Quest, now some three or so decades under way, represents a line of scholarship that departs from earlier scholarship in two important ways. First, among Third Questers there is a broad willingness to take the Gospels seriously as historical documents. This is not to say that everyone associated with the Third Quest would say that everything written in the Gospels reflects the historical reality. Rather, it is to say that the events and the plotline recorded in the Gospels have been increasingly seen as credible within a first-century Jewish context. Second, the Third Quest is also prepared, like no other time in the history of Jesus scholarship, to take on board the full weight of Jesus' Jewishness. Those writing within the vein of the Third Quest have generally made it a habit to compare Jesus' actions, ideas, and discernible intentions with other second-temple Jews; in doing so, they have found that this Jesus of the Gospels actually makes sense as a figure of history. The Third Quest says, "In order to understand Jesus, we must understand him as a Jew."

Yet for all this, there remain some who insist that Jesus was far more Greek than Jewish. Why does resistance to a Jewish Jesus linger? While there was a day in which the denial of Jesus' Judaism could have been chalked up to a rampant anti-Semitism, I don't think that is the case today. The atrocities of the Holocaust have brought about among Western thinkers a renewed sensitivity to Jewish concerns and anti-Semitism. There is no longer, as there once was, a cultural mandate to rid Jesus of his Judaism, not at least in the kinds of circles that write today's Jesus histories. Perhaps there are other theological or sociocultural reasons that some scholars prefer to fall back on a Graeco-Roman Jesus, but anti-Semitism simply cannot be said to figure in.

I suggest that at bottom the failure to grasp the Jewishness of Jesus and the failure to read the Gospels as historically reliable accounts of this same Jesus stem from a lack of imagination. It is not the inability to imagine a Jesus walking on water or raising the dead or being transfigured. Instead, it is a failure to imagine that the twentieth-century atrocities against the Jews were already being anticipated on a smaller scale in the first-century world of Jesus. The Jews of Jesus' day were a people who were sorely oppressed by Roman rule. They longed to be freed from those who politically, culturally, economically, and religiously lorded over them. The Jewish peasants of the Palestinian farmlands and the Jewish artisans of the towns were scratching out a living with the hope that some-day God would make good on his promises to deliver Israel. Such people wouldn't have much time for, or interest in, moral philoso-phers who merely spoke in platitudes. The desire of the nation was redemption from foreign bondage, and until that redemption was realized, Israel would continue to experience a holocaust of sorts. Any first-century Jew knew all too well the stories of how countless Jews suffered martyrdom at the hands of the Gentiles. This is the world in which Jesus, a very Jewish Jesus, came preaching the king-dom of God. It was a kingdom that he expected to be closely aligned with the continuing activity of his twelve disciples, who symbolically constituted the new Israel.

I submit that this is the best platform on which to understand the historical Jesus. Once this picture is in place, we are a good bit down the road in discerning whether or not Jesus' words have indeed been lost in transmission in the earliest stages. I will explain why this is so in our next chapter.

SIX

CAN YOU HEAR
ME NOW?

Matthew, in fact, is not exactly like Mark; Mark is not the same as Luke; or Luke as John; or John as Paul; or Paul as James. Just as scribes modified the words of the tradition, by sometimes putting these words "in other words," so too had the authors of the New Testament itself, telling their stories, giving their instructions, and recording their recollections by using their *own* words (not just the words they had heard), words that they came up with to pass along their message in ways that seemed most appropriate for the audience and the time and place for which they were writing.

—BART EHRMAN, *Misquoting Jesus*

The Good Friday service was progressing, and as promised, it was time to receive the Mass. I had never done this before (I couldn't really remember—with the exception of the previous night—even having been in a church before). What exactly were you supposed to do? Now I *was* beginning to get a little self-conscious.

These days, if I were to attend a Roman Catholic mass, I would not take part in the Eucharist. From the Roman Catholic perspective, to take the wafer would be to signify submission to the pope, and since I am Protestant by conviction, it would not make sense for me to do so. When as a minister in my denomination I serve communion, I ask those who have not yet put their faith in Christ to refrain. For Protestants, as for Orthodox and Catholics alike, eating the bread and drinking from the cup are also deeply symbolic acts; doing so is to say, "I belong to Jesus Christ." Christians of different stripes assign different significance to the Lord's Supper, but all agree that the Lord's Supper is a distinctively Christian activity, reserved for those in the church.

Of course, I didn't know any of this at the time. I thought that communion was served on a "Y'all come" basis. So I got up along with my roommate and joined the line of communicants, each making his or her way to the officiating priest. Not wanting to disrupt the service by asking my roommate what exactly would happen when it was my turn, I decided to keep my eye on the people ahead of me. Maybe by watching them, I could figure out what to do. Well, I did my best. But when I stepped up to take the wafer, the officiating priest's face nonetheless seemed to suggest that I mishandled the transaction. Whatever I did (I can't remember what it was), I certainly didn't fool the priest into thinking that I was a good Catholic who knew what he was doing.

By that point in my spiritual journey, I was familiar with Jesus' words to his disciples on the night he was betrayed: "And as they were eating, Jesus took bread, blessed and broke it, and gave it to them and said, 'Take, eat; this is My body'" (Mark 14:22). But I wasn't necessarily aware of the fact that the other two synoptic gospels, Matthew and Luke, also have this passage or something close to it. Nor was I aware that the apostle Paul, writing just over two decades after Jesus' death in his letter to the Corinthians, conveyed similar words in his instructions regarding the Lord's Supper. These are the words that Paul had "received" (1 Cor. 11:23–26). The so-called words of institution are attested in so many places and at such an early period that scholars cannot but concede their authenticity. Even the most skeptical of researchers will agree that the words regarding the bread and cup, which Mark and the other New Testament writers preserve, trace themselves back to the lips of Jesus.

Soon after Jesus' death, the Lord's Supper became the defining activity of Christians everywhere. It has endured as the universal focal point of Christian worship. Whatever distances have separated

Christian communities one from another down through the ages, the Lord's Supper has remained a unifying mark of the church. But this practice wasn't simply invented anonymously. What was occurring on that spring evening in 1982 in that church in Exeter was a recapitulation of an event that happened in the life of Jesus almost two thousand years earlier. From its origins, the Christian movement was one that looked back to Jesus and took his words with utmost seriousness.

Unfortunately, a good deal of twentieth-century scholarship on Jesus and the Gospels has not seen things quite that way. Leading the charge in this direction were three scholarly giants: Rudolf Bultmann (1884–1976), Karl L. Schmidt (1891–1956), and Martin Dibelius (1883–1947). Their major contributions all came out within a few years of one another, just after World War I.[1] Together, these three were the pioneers for what is called form criticism.

By definition, form criticism deals with the study of forms as they appear in the Gospels. Just as we constantly and quite unselfconsciously adopt different standard forms for different situations (consider, e.g., the typical ways of writing a thank-you note and a term paper), the earliest Christian community, so the earliest form critics thought, reduced the episodes of Jesus' life into certain forms. These forms reflected particular settings or problems going on in the early church. Consequently, the historically responsible critic must take the time to discern what in the gospel materials belongs to the gospel writer, what belongs to the early church, what belongs to the period of oral transmission, and what actually goes back to Jesus. For the form critics, a good portion of what is ascribed to Jesus in the Gospels does not actually go back to him. Rather, in many cases, Jesus' putative words are an invention of the early church as it sought to prove a point or settle a matter of disagreement that was rising up in its own ranks. Put differently, the Jesus tradition was again like a ball of many-colored string. Jesus may have started the ball, but then his immediate followers added on to it, and then the church and gospel writers made their contribution. Because there were different handlers of the tradition, who freely added to that tradition, this ball of string was rather difficult to untie.

Nevertheless, the form critics did their best to untangle the mess. One of their most prized tools in doing so was the criterion of multiple attestation. Here's how it works. If Jesus is recorded as saying or doing something in only one gospel, we cannot be very sure whether in fact that datum is authentic. However, if a particular saying or event is reproduced by several gospel writers, the historical stock of that saying or event goes up. The more shares, the higher the combined value. Better yet is when something is recorded by different gospels that have no literary relationship at all to one another.

The feeding of the five thousand, for example, occurs in all four gospels. Most scholars believe that this event was recorded in Mark, which was then in turn independently recorded by Matthew and Luke. This grants the feeding story a moderate degree of reliability, but the difference comes on recognizing that the fourth gospel, John, which most think to be independent of the synoptic gospels, also preserves this story. Compare this, say, with Jesus' telling of the parable of the good Samaritan, which only occurs in Luke. On the grounds of multiple attestation, the historical reliability of the feeding of the five thousand (what *really* happened with that bread and fish is another question) is fairly strong and certainly stronger than the reliability of the parable of the good Samaritan.

Another important criterion was that of double dissimilarity. The idea goes something like this. If we wish to know something about Jesus, we must first establish a minimum of Jesus material based on "critically assured results." One way to isolate this minimum is by looking back to the Judaism that surrounded Jesus and looking ahead to the Christianity that came after Jesus. If we find material that doesn't seem either to be Jewish or to fit the needs of the early church (Christian), this material can safely be attributed to Jesus. Where else could it come from? Thus, portions of Jesus' Sermon on the Mount, inasmuch as they are indelibly Jewish, cannot be ascribed with certainty to Jesus because they could just as well have hailed from an earlier Jewish tradition that entered the mix of the Jesus tradition. Likewise, when Jesus says, "If anyone desires to come after Me, let him deny himself, and take up his cross daily, and follow Me" (Luke 9:23), there is every reason to believe that it was the church and not Jesus himself who came up with this. After all, it is reasoned, how was Jesus to know he was going to die on a cross? (Never mind the very real possibility that Jesus knew full well that he might die for his cause and, equally, knew what penalty the Romans meted out to would-be messiahs.)

This approach to the Jesus tradition, made most popular by Norman Perrin (no relation to the present writer) in North America in the 1960s, would then become the methodological basis for the Jesus Seminar. The Jesus Seminar, founded several decades ago by the late Robert Funk, is a traveling colloquium of Jesus scholars who regularly meet to decide what Jesus actually said or didn't say. By using different colored beads (black, gray, pink, and red), the fellows of the seminar cast their vote as to what surely went back to Jesus, what may have gone back to Jesus, what probably did not go back to Jesus, and what definitely was not from Jesus. By applying form-critical methodologies, including the criteria of multiple attestation and double dissimilarity, the Jesus Seminar has turned out what may be considered a surprising portrait of Jesus. It is a Jesus who actually said very little of what is ascribed to him; it is also a Jesus who is not all that different from the non-Jewish, nineteenth-century portraits.

One might think that the results of the Jesus Seminar would give serious pause to those who insist on Jesus' Jewishness. But I'm not so sure. First of all, the Jesus Seminar has inherited and failed to modify the basic assumption of the form critics that the early Christians were completely disinterested in the historical Jesus. Bultmann and his colleagues at Marburg University were operating out of a philosophical outlook that was decidedly existentialist, Heideggerian to be exact. According to Heidegger (1889–1976), personhood has less to do with objective verities outside of oneself in time and space, and more to do with authentic self-realization through the power of choice. If the typical nineteenth-century scholar had created Jesus after his own image, then Bultmann merely repeats the mistake, this time by recreating the early church in the image of the faculty at Marburg. "Surely," Bultmann seems to say, "what the early church cared about was not the historical Jesus but the reenactment of what Jesus was all about: daring to choose."

In response, we might say that this line of thinking, while common enough in early twentieth-century German lecture halls, does not seem to present itself naturally in the ancient sources. Instead, if Jesus was Jewish and, as the sources imply, his first followers were

Jewish, we would expect the early church to take a great interest in his words and deeds. Ancient Judaism always took its cues from the past and took pains to remember the past so that future generations would not forget. In short, Bultmann is able to superimpose his modern philosophical apparatus on the early church only by willfully overlooking the fact that the early church was essentially Jewish, and if essentially Jewish, then also deeply interested in history, even the history of Jesus.

In the previous chapter I argued that Jesus' movement declared not only a break with the existent temple authorities but also the inauguration of a new temple reality that stood in continuity with the temple that Herod had built. Jesus himself was the hinge on which salvation history turned; Jesus himself marked the transition between Herod's temple and the new temple community. This sense of continuity implies that the first Christians would have been interested in not only establishing a historical continuity with the Israel that had gone before (as becomes clear in the very first chapter of the New Testament, Matthew 1) but also setting down in oral and written form what Jesus did and said. Jesus could not have been seen as anything other than the primary reinterpreter of the Hebrew scriptures. This being the case, what he had to say about the scriptures and their working out in the life of the new temple community would have been of utmost significance.

Unfortunately, we know almost nothing about how first-century Jews preserved oral tradition. But we do know how Jews of the post-temple period (post AD 70), especially from the second and third century, treated oral traditions. In 1961 Birger Gerhardsson published a groundbreaking book called *Memory and Manuscript* (Uppsala). Here Gerhardsson sought to refute the old form-critical notion that the traditioning of Jesus material was fairly wild and erratic. Examining the practice of ancient rabbis, Gerhardsson found that in post-temple Judaism the Jewish teachers would have their students learn their lessons by rote. In other words, whatever the rabbi taught, it was the disciple's obligation to write it down or memorize it on the spot. Then after repetition at home the disciple would have committed his master's teachings to long-term memory. If this is the closest we can get to first-century Palestianian Judaism, Gerhardsson argued, then this is also our best guess as to how Jesus passed on his teachings. In this case, the words of Jesus have been preserved almost exactly as he uttered them.

Gerhardsson's thesis dealt a powerful blow to the way most Jesus scholars were accustomed to thinking of oral transmission. Not surprisingly, critics were swift to rise up and respond. A few of their criticisms are quite sound. In the first place, it was charged that Gerhardsson's methodology was anachronistic. If we assume that post-temple Judaism was a very different thing from second-temple Judaism (Jesus' setting), then how legitimate is it to assume that the practices of the former were also practices of the latter? Second, if indeed the disciples learned everything by rote, word for word, then why do we have so much variation within the Gospels themselves as to what Jesus said? There are indeed a few places where the Gospels have parallel passages that match up word for word. But then there are other places where there is a wild variation in Jesus' words. Somehow, Gerhardsson's account seems to presuppose a setting that is *too* controlled.

At any rate, these criticisms do not change the fact that

Gerhardsson has demonstrated that post-temple Judaism was, in fact, extremely conservative when it came to passing on authoritative teaching. If this is so, then even if the mechanics of transmission were different in Jesus' case, it should still be surmised that the normal practice of Jewish tradents was at least to preserve the thrust of their master's words. Jesus' role as a Jewish teacher gives us grounds for inferring that his disciples saw themselves as responsible for transmitting his words accurately.

But Jesus was not just a Jewish teacher, a rabbi, for he was also a Jewish *movement founder*. The particular goal of this movement, I have been arguing, was to secure a new and true temple for Israel; it was to be a temple made up of people, not bricks and mortar. Much of Jesus' ministry can, in fact, be explained by this aim. His dispensing the forgiveness of sins apart from the established temple cultus (Mark 2:1–12), his public association with those who were unclean and therefore personae non gratae among the temple authorities (Mark 2:13–22), his reconfiguring of the temple calendar (Mark 2:23–28), his making the unclean clean (Mark 5:1–41)—all such activities show that Jesus was up to something much larger than randomly going around doing good. His goal was nothing less than to build a newly defined temple around himself and his disciples.

In this case the Twelve were not simply casual onlookers; they were integral to Jesus' ministry. He called them to himself (Mark 3:13–21) in order that they might do the very things that he had been doing (Mark 6:7–13). In fact, the very act of sending the disciples out meant that, from that point on, Jesus was establishing them as authoritative spokespersons. The teachings of Jesus were to be the very foundation of their missionary message (Matt. 10:27). In order to represent their master faithfully, the disciples would have been obliged to note well and represent what, in fact, Jesus was teaching. Quite apart from their missionary activity, the disciples would be forced now and again to answer on behalf of their master (Mark 2:16). Surely it would have been impractical for them to do so apart from some firm, agreed-upon sense among the Twelve as to what Jesus really said.

Given the many times Jesus predicted his death (and he would have had to be grossly naïve not to consider that death would be a likely outcome of his activity), the disciples also would have understood that their master's words stood a good chance of outlasting the master. Jesus speaks very matter-of-factly as though this was the case (Mark 8:34–38; 13:31). There would in fact come a day, Jesus intimates, when once he was gone, the disciples would have to gather his words in their memories with the Spirit's help (John 14:25–27). Over the course of his ministry, Jesus entrusted his words to his disciples, for he knew they would need them if they were to be faithful to the vision he had for Israel. In sum, Jesus' self-consciousness as the founder of a new temple movement implies that the Twelve had a crucial role as witnesses and leaders in the unfolding of Jesus' purposes; this point was sufficiently recognized by the disciples themselves even while Jesus was still alive (Mark 10:35–37).

Clearly, then, the destiny of the early Christians would rise or fall on the disciples' ability to vouchsafe that their movement, and their movement alone, constituted the visible embodiment of Yahweh's continued faithfulness to Israel. Whether this was indeed the case in turn depended completely on the person of Jesus and on whether Jesus was indeed God's appointed Messiah, as they had claimed. As Messiah, Jesus would have been interpreter par excellence of the Hebrew scriptures and the history of Israel. Jesus' words (and deeds) were therefore the glue of Christian conviction. For the early church to have lost them in transmission would have spelled a complete undermining of what Jesus had been aiming for all along. Jesus and Jesus alone was the bridge between the old and the new. Jesus' followers had deep and abiding interest in getting the bridge down right.

Therefore, as historians we are right to assume on general grounds that we have *not* lost Jesus' words in transmission. The words of Jesus, as recorded in the canonical gospels, are to the best of our knowledge his words indeed. Despite the protestations of certain scholars to the contrary, the scope and substance of Jesus' words must be presumed to go back to Jesus himself.

But with this statement comes two qualifications. In the first place, because I have set forth my conclusion as a general principle, this does not *prove* that in each and every instance we have the words of Jesus. Here we must remember the limits of history. What history cannot do is prove that Jesus said this or didn't say that. History cannot *prove* anything.[2] What history can do is offer a plausible reconstruction of matters past. My claim here is simply that among the range of historical models on offer, the most plausible one of all is that which takes Jesus' words, as recorded in the Gospels, with utmost seriousness. Unless there are compelling reasons for not assigning certain words to Jesus, we should assume the master said it. We can hear him now.

Second, this is not to say that the Gospels consistently contain the *ipsissima verba* (very words) of Jesus. Technically speaking, because Jesus spoke Aramaic and the Gospels almost always record his words in Greek, we have almost no account of his ipsissima verba.³ What we generally have instead is his *ipsissima vox* (very voice). This means that when the gospel writers represented what Jesus had to say, they did so with some stylistic freedom. As anyone who has done translating knows, some degree of wordsmithing is necessary in moving from one language to another. To insist on a word-for-word equivalency is usually to end up with nonsense rather than meaningful sense. Moreover, because the gospel writers had certain literary goals as well as certain audiences, this, too, might cause them to tweak the words of Jesus as appropriate. Such "tweaking" was no doubt necessitated by the gospel writers' sensitivity to their immediate audiences. There also must have been a number of word choices induced by linguistic, stylistic, grammatical, narrative, cultural, and theological considerations.

In any event, I believe that the disciples saw themselves as having heard Jesus faithfully and as the appointed means by which others would hear Jesus faithfully after them. And because they wished to be faithful, they chose at times to re-represent Jesus' words exactly as he spoke them; at other times, they chose to give the thrust of Jesus' words in their own words. (When we give an account of a dialogue of, say, an interchange that happened at the office, we do the same thing without thinking about it, and no one thinks the less of us for it.) There are no credible historical reasons for believing that the disciples always and everywhere preserved Jesus' *precise* words; nor, on the other hand, is there evidence that they were prepared to spin sayings out of whole cloth.

Some will undoubtedly be scandalized by the former statement, but for good historical reasons, they need not be. Others will be scandalized by the latter statement, but for good theological reasons, they need not be. When I look back to taking communion at my first Good Friday service, it never troubled me that Jesus failed to specify what kind of bread was to be broken in remembrance of him. Neither did it bother me that he did not specify the type of wine, whether merlot or cabernet. The fact that he was less than thoroughly specific in breaking the bread and sharing wine is no grounds for invalidating the thrust of what he was doing that night two thousand years ago. Jesus' words of institution over the Lord's Supper spoke loud and clear, even if we don't have a copy of his wine list, even if we don't have the recipe for the bread he was holding in his hands. Communication need not be exhaustive in order to be effective.

Even in my very limited theological and historical understanding, I could hear what Jesus was saying. He was saying that he had done something profound for me. If his bread was his body, then his body was given for me. He was broken for me. He died for me. He loved me. Within minutes of returning to my seat, I was beginning to realize all of this. It was a joyful moment. At that moment, too, I was beginning to believe something. I was beginning to believe that he was the Christ, the Son of the living God.

But in my mind I still had questions.

SEVEN

THE EVANGELIST'S HAND

The idea that Luke changed the text before him—in this case the Gospel of Mark—does not put him in a unique situation among the early Christian authors. This, in fact, is what all the writers of the New Testament did—along with all the writers of all the Christian literature outside the New Testament, indeed writers of every kind everywhere. . . . Each of them, in a sense, was changing the "texts" he inherited.

—BART EHRMAN, *Misquoting Jesus*

My favorite roommate and I were wending our way back to the dormitory in the night darkness. I can't recall whether we spoke much or, if we did, what we talked about. I have no memory of talking about the effect of the worship or encountering the divine or anything like that. My earlier intimation that Jesus was, in fact, the Son of God was intensely personal, and I was not about to share it. Who knows what Roomie (or others he might tell) would think? Like Peter, I felt I had witnessed a kind of transfiguration and I was being charged to keep silent. In Peter's case it was Jesus himself who was forbidding the disciples from reporting their encounter. In my case, it was a voice within: my fear of appearing odd, coupled with a prior and unexamined assumption that religion was supposed to be a personal, private affair—nothing more.

How different our impressions must have been! Here he was, a confirmed Roman Catholic Christian who would probably be the first to confess that he did not always act in a way that was consistent with the teachings of his church, but who at the time had somehow come to terms with the inconsistency. Perhaps it simply came down to the fact that while Roman Catholicism had been in his background, it had never become his religion in the proper sense. If religion is by definition a comprehensive way of making sense of life, a configuring of *all* one's activities, perceptions, and thoughts, then there was in reality some other worldview, something other than Roman Catholicism, that was holding his thought world together. Sometimes people can even be conscientiously religious, but the claims of their religious tradition are not what give plausibility and structure to the rest of their existence. How he might relate his attendance at this Good Friday service to the rest of his life, I'm not quite sure. I wish I had asked.

As for me, I was on the outside looking in. Everything was new and fresh and strange. It was almost as if I were a tourist in a foreign country whose language I could barely understand. And yet there was something attractive about the language. It drew me, not because it sounded exotic but because there was an inherent beauty in what it said. There was a certain aesthetic appeal, in other words, in the story behind the wooden figure hanging on the rear wall of the church. Exuding an elusive beauty, the life and words of Jesus were drawing me.

And yet given who I was, it could only be the experience of beauty on my terms. I was not about to allow a religious experience to take over my life. Coming down from the mountaintop, I felt it was time to move on to the next experience. Real life had to go on. Maybe my roommate was interested in tracking down a couple of six-packs with me that night?

However the two of us may have recapped our church experience on our way back to campus, there is no doubt that our personal perceptions of the evening's events bore mutual similarities and differences. When we saw Jesus on the cross, when we heard

Jesus' words in Scripture during the homily, when we went up to take the Eucharist—our take on what was going on could not help but be shaped by who we were as people. While we certainly could have agreed on the bare facts of what happened during that course of the service, our interpretations would have necessarily differed. Events in themselves are objective things, but the recollection of events necessarily introduces subjective or personal elements.

It should come as no surprise that the same dynamic applies when it comes to the four gospel writers. The four evangelists (Matthew, Mark, Luke, and John) write about the same Jesus, but that which they seek to achieve—their literary, theological, and pastoral motivations—is different. This is important to stress, especially because our default mode as twenty-first-century westerners is to presume that the gospel writers worked from a narrowly "scientific," post-Enlightenment point of view, as if in the act of writing their stories, they might be heard to mutter to themselves, "Just the facts, man. Just the facts." But this would be a mistake. It would be a mistake, in other words, to assume that the gospel writers, much like, say, a satellite weather camera, were simply interested in the objective gathering and rendering of data.

Returning to a metaphor I used earlier, I would submit that the four evangelists are less like satellite cameras and more like portrait painters, artists who wish to render their subject faithfully and, in order to do so, paint in their own way, with their own brushstrokes, and for their own audience. And as you might find in an art class with the model posing in the center of the room, each "gospel artist" has his own very different angle. Imagine in such a class what would happen if at the end of the day the art instructor were to receive a dozen renderings of the model, all of them more or less identical. What would she think? "What is going on here?" might be the first words out of her mouth. "This isn't art. This is plagiarism!" Different vantage points, different lighting, different personal interests, different temperaments and experiences, different purposes for the painting—all these conspire to ensure that the paintings themselves will each deal with the same subject in a unique way.

But in weighing the claim that the gospel writers *changed* the text of one or more of the earlier gospels, we have to be clear as to what is really meant by the claim. For now, two points need to be clarified. In considering two gospel writers, an earlier one and a later one who makes changes on the earlier one's text, we must first ask this: where the later gospel writer has in effect changed the wording of the prior text, is the change substantive? Second, if the change is substantive, what is this later gospel writer's relationship to the events that both he and the prior text report? Is the later gospel writer's only access to the events through the earlier gospel, or does he have independent access that might cause him to represent matters differently? That "Luke changed the text before him" I am willing to grant. But without clarification on these two points, it is all too easy to smuggle in certain unwarranted assumptions, and once these are on board, Luke will soon enough be relieved of his role as historian and his gospel redirected to a destination he never intended.

Consider, by way of analogy, a hypothetical situation in which I am an off-duty police officers involved in a multiple-vehicle car accident. When other police officers show up, it is somehow assumed that I saw the whole thing and I am asked to write up my own report of the accident when I get back to the station. When I do return to the station, I first decide to look at someone else's narrative report to see what he said about the accident. Then I proceed to write my own narrative report and do so knowing that it is in some ways very close to the others' reports but also in some ways different.

If, on the one hand, I write a narrative report that is a verbatim repetition of a report I read earlier in the morning and adds absolutely nothing new from my perspective, I would simply be wasting everyone's time. Why, it might be asked, did I even bother writing a report if I was simply intent on copying someone else's? On the other hand, if my report is extremely different from the earlier report, then questions of accuracy would be raised and incompatibilities would have to be resolved. Drastic differences between my narrative account and that of another driver would mean that either he or I would be the source of misinformation. A traffic court judge who hopes to resolve the case quickly would hope not for identical narrative reports (which would suggest collusion) but a kind of middle-road agreement between the reports. If there were only minor differences between my accident report and those of others, the reports together would likely be viewed as being in essential agreement.

Now let's just say that the case comes to court. The judge reads my very long accident report narrative along with the others. He tells me that the reports are generally in agreement but there are differences worth probing. Toward getting to the bottom of those differences, the court would naturally be interested in revisiting the question as to how much I saw. If, on the one hand, I can credibly affirm that I was in a good position to see the whole crash from start to finish, then this will influence the way my report is read. If, on the other hand, it comes out that I was actually playing with my car stereo at the moment of impact, only heard and felt the crash, then figured out what happened when I read the narrative report of another driver, then in having substantively changed that narrative I am immediately shown up for having at best misled the court and at worst perjured myself.

And so it is simply not satisfactory to say, "Luke changed the text before him," and leave it at that. Assuming "the text before him" has at least some historical value to it, we find that the statement prompts two sorts of historical questions. First, it begs the question as to whether the changes in view constitute true discrepancies. Second, it potentially raises the question as to whether Luke had sources other than "the text before him" that might justify the changes. More to the point, the proposition "Luke changed the text before him" either forces more questions than it answers or presumes it already has certain answers.

In sorting out the first issue (Does the change in wording from one gospel to another constitute a true discrepancy?), the real trick here is in determining just what we mean by "true discrepancy." My experience in these discussions is that certain readers of the Gospels are very quick to slide from the notion of "difference" or "change" to the notion of "contradiction." But of course neither "difference" nor "change" means contradiction, at least not necessarily.

Returning one more time to our art class illustration, let's say that the model who is posing for this art class has a barely discernible mole on her face. And let's say that one art student includes the mole in his rendering and another student does not. Would you necessarily say that the latter student, in omitting the mole, was *contradicting* the former student or the facts? Probably not. Either the mole was there or the mole was not there. But if one artist decides to bring it out and draw attention to it, while the other can barely see it, regards it as unimportant, and neglects to render it, their decisions should not be construed as a barometer of their desire to present a true-to-the-facts portrait. Since even the most realistic representation requires selectivity and personal judgment, no two such representations (if they are true representations and not just copies of another) will present the same object in the same way.

And yet there is a remarkable continuity in how the evangelists present Jesus. They depict him as the one who came proclaiming the kingdom of God. Jesus said that this kingdom was near and spoke frequently about it, largely through mysterious stories called parables. He taught about what life would be like for those who chose the kingdom way. He also taught about himself and his mission. And besides everything he said, he gave visible expression to his words by his miraculous acts of healing, feeding, walking on water, and raising the dead—to mention a few. He called to himself twelve disciples, ate regularly with "sinners," and butted heads with the temple leadership of the day. Eventually, his conflict with the temple authorities brought him to trial, then to a Roman cross on which he died. He then rose from the dead. Despite differences, the plotline of the Gospels, their basic message as to Jesus' identity and mission, is of one voice. Any discussion of the differences between the Gospels, in order to be fair-minded, must be set against the basic recognition that Matthew, Mark, Luke, and John are far more similar in what they purport than they are different.

The other point that needs to be emphasized here is that difference does not entail contradiction. Nor does "change" mean contradiction. Perhaps that is obvious enough. But sometimes even highly trained New Testament scholars can be slippery in their use of language. In the blink of an eye, when you're not looking, "change" suddenly implicitly morphs into "contradiction." So let's be clear. You have *change* if Mark says "A" and Luke says "B." You have *contradiction* if Mark says "A" and Luke says "not A." Between the four gospels there are many points of difference, to be sure, and sometimes these differences create tensions, even serious tensions (that is, points of substantive disagreement). But if we use our terms properly, then we would be hard-pressed to find any one place in which the Gospels contradict each other.

Toward understanding a few of these differences, we might take the parable of the mustard seed as an example. According to Mark 4:31, Jesus says, the kingdom of God is like a mustard seed "sown on the *ground* [*gē*]" (emphasis mine). According to Matthew 13:31, Jesus refers to it as a seed "which a man took and sowed in his *field* [*agros*]" (emphasis mine). And according to Luke 13:19, Jesus says "which a man took and put in his *garden* [*kēpos*]" (emphasis mine). We can't be sure which word Jesus would have used in the Aramaic. We have some ideas, but again we cannot be certain. Mark may certainly have had his reasons for choosing "ground" (*gē*), for he seemed interested in weaving this particular term in and out of his gospel (Mark 2:10; 4:1; et. al.). Matthew also seems to have his reasons for preferring *agros*: it ties in perfectly with the surrounding parables that also necessarily involve a "field" (namely the parable of the weeds [Matt. 13:24–30] and the parable of the hidden treasure [Matt. 13:44]). Finally, if Luke's gospel was written to a wider audience that included a number of urban Romans, it would have made sense for him to use "garden" for the benefit of his many readers who didn't have much experience with agriculture but who knew well enough what it was like to plant veggies in a small backyard plot. This is no contradiction between the three gospels. The fact that the gospel writers employ different terms to convey the same basic concept (the place in which you plant the seed) simply means that they are using different brushstrokes to depict one and the same reality. Here you might chalk up the variations between the three gospels to the evangelists' literary or rhetorical sensitivity. Were there space, we might consider countless other instances where the evangelist's hand has gently touched up his particular presentation.

But this explanation also has its limits. My approach to explaining Jesus' divergent word choice in the parable of the mustard seed does not help us much in sorting through the differing accounts as to who came to Jesus' tomb on the first Easter morning. In each of the four gospels, we have a resurrection account involving women who witness the empty tomb. According to Matthew 28:1, Mary Magdalene and the "other Mary" went to the tomb on Easter morning. According to Mark 16:1, the women who came included Mary Magdalene, Mary the mother of James, and Salome. As Luke 24:10 reports it, it was Mary Magdalene, Joanna, Mary the mother of James, "and the other women with them." John 20:1 only mentions Mary Magdalene.

Assuming that there is a core historical element to this episode (that several days after Jesus' death *someone* went out and had a not-your-everyday-kind-of experience), there are a few strategies a historian can employ to resolve the discrepant reports. In the first instance, if we assume for the sake of argument that Matthew and Luke independently used Mark, and John had access to all three (in addition to who knows how many oral and written sources), then we *might* be able to work out a kind of theory as to why Luke and

Matthew made the changes they did on Mark and why John, using all three, made the changes he did. Mary Magdalene seems to be the constant factor. But perhaps Mark wanted to make sure the scene included Salome, and Luke for his part wanted to make sure Joanna was included. Maybe there were literary and/or theological reasons for doing do, or even personal reasons. Luke, for example, having already mentioned this very Joanna earlier in his narrative (Luke 8:2), may be drawing a link to her role as described earlier in the book. But whatever motivations Luke, Matthew, and John may have had in changing Mark's story, the very fact that they changed the story puts them in a position analogous to a policeman who didn't see his own accident and then files an accident report that consciously reworks the report written by someone who actually knew what happened. In other words, if Mark is the only link to the past, then any changes on Mark by later evangelists would constitute a rewriting of history.

Throughout his argument, Ehrman leaves the strong impression that Luke "overwrote" Mark (as one overwrites an outdated word processing file) and thereby rewrote history without having legitimate grounds for doing so. But this view of Luke works only if we assume that he was utterly dependent on Mark and had no way of comparing Mark against other sources. According to Luke's own testimony, there were other written accounts in circulation (Luke 1:1), but he also claims to have received his information directly from eyewitnesses (v. 2), people who had personal contact with Jesus. Unless Luke is misleading us on this score (there is no good reason to suspect he is), we have to believe that Luke in fact did not see himself as changing Mark so much as creating a new account that was a synthesis of Mark and other sources. Included among these sources were personal reminiscences of those who walked with Jesus. In this case when we come to Luke's handling of the women at the tomb, we are best served if we believe that both Mark and Luke were, despite their differences, true to the facts. Mark had his sources on which he drew; Luke had his sources on which he drew, not least of which was Mark itself. The best surmise is not that Mark or Luke or the eyewitnesses were confused as to who was there on Easter morning (it's hard to imagine the early church becoming so quickly muddled about the circumstances of such an extraordinary event); rather, the best surmise is that there was a contingent of named and unnamed women who went to the tomb first thing in the morning. Mark mentions some names, while Luke happens to mention other names. There is partial overlap, but there is also difference. The difference need not be understood as reflecting poorly on Mark or Luke. As long as Luke had independent access to testimony about the events of Jesus' life, which is precisely what he claims, he did not so much change the text as synthesize it with what he knew from other sources.

So much for so many of the diverging details of Jesus' life, but what about his words? When it comes to comparing the words of Jesus as recorded in the different gospels, sometimes we have a very different account as to what Jesus' words actually were. In many cases, I believe we don't have two disparate accounts of the same speech or sermon; rather, more often than not we have two accounts of two or more different speeches. For example, when we compare Matthew's Sermon on the Mount with Luke's Sermon on the Plain, we find very similar wording in places but also very different wordings. In my view (although this is debated), these two sermons are not derived from one and the same sermon in the life of Jesus. Instead, if Jesus, like any sought-after preacher today, repeated his sermons on numerous occasions, we would expect the words of his various sermons to be handed down with different wording. Differences between the gospel texts here may be not so much a function of changes wrought by the gospel writers, but a function of the diversity of traditions in the living memory of the first generation of believers.

Having said all this, I also need to say that despite these principles for working through the Gospels, historical problems remain. Many of Jesus' speeches and certain events may be explained by multiple occurrences of similar sermons or events in the life of Jesus. But there are instances where it simply cannot be the case that three gospel writers reflect on three different events. Presumably there was only one time when the disciples' boat was virtually swamped and Jesus stilled the storm. But there are differences between the accounts. In Matthew 8:25 the disciples say, "Lord, save us!" Mark 4:38 has the disciples saying, "Teacher, do You not care that we are perishing?" Luke 8:24 reads, "Master, Master, we are perishing!" So what did the disciples actually say to Jesus—exactly? How did they address him? It seems far-fetched to say that three gospel writers record three separate verbatim statements made during the moment of crisis. While it is not impossible that all three words (Lord, Teacher, and Master) were heard at one time or another in the midst of the chaos, it does seem like a rather unwieldy explanation that each of these gospel writers also happens to record one title for the sake of the record. Also, Matthew has Jesus rebuking the disciples before calming the storm, whereas Mark and Luke recount Jesus rebuking the disciples *after* the miracle. Which happened first: the rebuking of the disciples or the calming of the storm? Or was Jesus' rebuking of the disciples more of a prolonged event than the Gospels at first blush lead us to imagine?

There are times, I think, when as historians, we make our best effort to harmonize the data and make our best guess as to what really happened behind the text of the Gospels. There are other times, however, when perhaps we are better served by simply saying, "I pass." I do think that the four gospels pass muster as coherent history, but this is not the same thing as saying that we fully understand the particulars of all the events the Gospels purport to tell. Sometimes the better part of wisdom is knowing when to plead ignorance. Sometimes we need to give ourselves permission to not have all the answers.

With an ironical twinkle in his eye, the existentialist philosopher Albert Camus once defined the world as the place where there are all answers and no questions. When certain conservative readers of Scripture adopt a posture that says, "We have all the answers, and there are no more questions," others of us are rightfully suspicious. The last time I checked, it was not our job to have all the answers—it was God's. The call of the Christian is to give a credible and coherent account of a historically based faith; it is an account that leaves room for ambiguity and even mystery. The choice to assign certain difficult matters to the realm of mystery, even historical mystery, stems not from a failure of conviction or evangelical nerve. Rather, it is born of the recognition that our being Christian does not also require us to be rationalists.

EIGHT

GOSPEL TRUTH
OR GOSPEL TRUTHS?

If they [the gospel writers] are not saying the same thing, it is not legitimate to assume they are—for example, by taking what Mark says, and taking what Luke says, then taking what Matthew and John say and melding them all together, so that Jesus says and does *all* the things that each of the Gospel writers indicates. Anyone who interprets the Gospels this way is not letting each author have his own say; anyone who does this is not reading what the author wrote in order to understand his message; anyone who does this is not reading the Gospels themselves—he or she is making up a *new* Gospel consisting of the four in the New Testament, a *new* Gospel that is not like any of the ones that have come down to us.

—BART EHRMAN, *Misquoting Jesus*

The New England winter seemed to be dragging on. They usually do. Along with Latin, Greek, and poetry writing, I was also continuing on in Mr. Mac's comparative religions class. We had come to Judaism. Judaism, Huston Smith noted in our textbook, was different from the Eastern religions in that it took history seriously. That also may explain why, Smith went on to say, the Jews have historically contributed far beyond their numbers to the social, economic, and political betterment of humanity. Little did I know at the time that in learning about history for Judaism, I was laying the groundwork for some of the most fundamental concepts of Christianity.

The assigned text for that portion of the course was an old, out-of-print book called *Awake, Awake to Do the Work of the Creator*. It was a fine, hardback book with golden Hebrew letters on the white front cover of the sleeve. The book was a semi-autobiographical account of what it was like to grow up in an orthodox Jewish home. As I read, I came to feel that there was a certain orderliness to the orthodox Jewish way of life, a rhyme and a rhythm. There was also a core belief in a personal God, very close to the glimpse I caught of the personal God peering out at me from the pages of the New Testament.

I remember how one day the school wrestling team, of which I was a part, was hosting a meet. The team got dressed in their gear then gathered in a lounge area before taking to the mat. In my gym bag I packed among other things my copy of *Awake, Awake to Do the Work of the Creator*. I remember how one of my teammates chided me for "studying" when I should have been thinking about the upcoming match, getting mentally focused and psyched up. But what he didn't know and what I couldn't really explain to him was that at the time reading about Judaism was my way of getting psyched up. It was like a prayer book. I thought if the God of Israel could help Jesus and help the Jews, maybe he also could help me while I was going into the third period so tired that I could hardly see. I don't think I have ever been in such good shape since my senior year in high school. But even so I knew there were opponents out there who could overpower me. The fear of losing a match drove me to seek out a higher power.

I was practicing Buddhist meditation at the time, and I would continue to experiment with it for another several years. But in reading about Judaism and the sect that stemmed from it, Christianity, I realized that these two related religions had at least this one thing clearly over the Eastern religions: while the Eastern idea is that suffering is an illusion, both Judaism and Christianity take suffering seriously. If Buddha thought that suffering was not real, then it only goes to show that Buddha never belonged to a high school or collegiate wrestling team. If Buddha didn't think suffering was real, then what exactly do you go up and tell your neighbor who is beating the tar out of his wife with a baseball bat? "Have a good day"? This was something I could never get my head around. Eventually, Buddhism's refusal to wrestle with suffering led me to see Eastern religion as escapist.

The Jews, partially because they took history seriously, also took suffering seriously. For Judaism, suffering was a self-defining component of life. Growing up outside of New York City, where synagogues were not complete oddities, I had the impression that to be conscious of one's Jewishness was also to be conscious of suffering. Suffering had redemptive possibilities and meaning. Suffering, when bad things happen to people's bodies and psyches, could pave the way to a knowledge of God. According to the Eastern religions, not to mention a good bit of the Western philosophical tradition indebted to Plato, the body was always getting in the way, but it was quite different for Jews and Christians. If Plato and Buddha said that in the school of God the body was like the troublesome kid who would pull the fire alarm just when the class was settling down for its lessons, in the Judeo-Christian tradition the body *was* the classroom. Knowledge of God did not occur apart from the body. Bodily harms and bodily cares, the "slings and arrows of outrageous fortune," as Shakespeare put it, are not a distraction from the truth. They are the script through which an apprehension of the truth takes shape.

I kept reading the Gospels in those days. Having been at this gospel-reading thing for a year, I had long since realized that some of these stories about Jesus actually repeat themselves in different gospels. *Why would you have all this repetition between the four gospels?* I finally wondered. *What's the point? Wouldn't the Bible be more efficient and less wordy if there was only one gospel instead of four?*

I was not aware of it at the time, but in retrospect it occurs to me that my question about the redundancy of the Gospels was actually related to the issue of how truth is mediated. In order to explain why, it is necessary to go back not to the Bible but to a church father who served as the bishop of Lyons (in southern France) toward the end of the second century, a man by the name of Irenaeus. Lest you think that you wouldn't have minded being bishop in the sunny south of France, you should know a little bit about Irenaeus's situation. In the first place he was taking on leadership over a church that had been undergoing severe persecution for its faith. Months before his coming, many Christians in the region had been hacked to pieces by Romans. Their crime? Belief in a bodily resurrection. The Christians knew exactly what they could do if they wished to avoid prison, torture and death. All they had to do was renounce their belief that they would be raised bodily in the future. But for these Christians from Lyons, prison, torture, and death were preferable to renouncing that which held their faith together: God's reestablishing the true people of God in incorruptible bodily form in a renewed creation.

Another problem was confronting Irenaeus as well: the proliferation of gospels. He knew Matthew, Mark, Luke, and John. But he also knew and was distressed by other so-called gospels, including the *Gospel of Judas*, which has just fairly recently been rediscovered. Toward setting the record straight, Irenaeus writes that there could only be four:

The Gospels could not possibly be either more or less in number than they are. Since there are four zones of the world in which we live, and four principal winds, while the Church is spread over all the earth, and the pillar and foundation of the Church is the gospel, and the Spirit of life, it fittingly has four pillars, everywhere breathing out incorruption and revivifying men.[1]

This, in a nutshell, is Irenaeus's rationale for why there should be four gospels—no more, no less. In his book Ehrman cites the famed quote and cannot resist commenting. With a thinly veiled tone of sarcasm, he writes, "In other words, four corners of the earth, four winds, four pillars—and necessarily, then four Gospels."[2] Ehrman apparently doesn't think there's much sense to the bishop of Lyons' argument. He is not alone: countless other New Testament scholars are equally quick to shake their heads at what they think is a frivolous, arbitrary argument.

But we should be careful not to be hasty in criticizing something we may not quite understand. I believe that Irenaeus has largely been misunderstood, at least by contemporary critics. I also believe that in order to offer a fair assessment of his remarks, we must understand them within the context of his larger argument against the Gnostics, which relies mightily on his doctrines of creation and incarnation. As I read the bishop of Lyons, I read him as making a rather profound point about the mediation of truth. As he sees it, if the story of Jesus Christ is to be communicated at all, it must be conveyed through a plurality of stories. The plurality of stories must not only reflect the complexity of Christ's person but also parallel the complexity of the four corners of creation itself.

In Irenaeus's mind, this is one of the things that sets Christianity apart from Gnosticism. For the Gnostic believers, who were precommitted to the Platonic notion that truth was contained strictly in ideas (as opposed to things like a God-man's body), revelation about the truth of the universe was passed down orally through the line of Gnostic believers. Most Gnostic systems had a myth that explained how the world came into existence. And for most of these Gnostic myths, the creation of the world was akin to an accident at a nuclear reactor. Somehow, some bumbling fool, whom the Jews call Yahweh, their Creator God, got it into his head to create this fine mess we now call creation. "Who," the Gnostics wondered, "but some kind of cosmic buffoon or jerk would create a world where people caught colds, chariots broke down regularly, and disastrous typhoons occurred?" Since a cosmic jerk was behind the cosmos, there must be a higher god who transcended physical materiality. And if there was, that god would surely want to communicate with his own elect, those among humanity who know that they deserve better. And in communicating, the same true god would not stoop to use such a filthy, fragile thing as the human body. Instead, according to the Gnostics, it was ideas that saved people. If you get the idea, if you have the right knowledge, you are saved. Of course, "being saved" and "salvation" mean very different things for Gnostics and Christians. For the former, these concepts mean a restoration of self-knowledge and a return to divine self-consciousness; for the latter, they mean a heart-soul-mind-body participation in a divinely initiated and divinely wrought cosmic renewal.

The Gnostic vision of human existence is paradoxical. On the one hand, Gnostics taught that we as humans were higher in status than the Creator God. After all, we would certainly know better than to do such a silly thing as call a physical world into being. On the other hand, human existence was also pretty bleak because humanity could not help but have a deeply antagonistic posture to the world. Jim Morrison, the lead singer for the Doors, expresses the Gnostic vision perfectly when he sings:

> Into this house we're born,
> Into this world we're thrown.[3]

For Morrison, as for the Gnostics and for plenty of people living today, once you attain the truth of who you are, you have the hope of transcending this world. In the meantime, you are in alien territory.

While Irenaeus would undoubtedly object to the Gnostic idea that knowledge saves, he also would object to the Gnostics' aversion to the material world and the God who stands behind his world. In the first chapter of Genesis, we read that God made the heavens and earth. At the end of it all, he declared it "good." In essence, Judaism and Christianity teach that creation is good and is not to be scoffed at. Yes, things go awry when sin enters the world through Adam and Eve, but this does not render the physical world intrinsically evil, for God has his heart set on redeeming the physical world. Against the Gnostics who would say, "The idea saves," Irenaeus says, "No, Jesus Christ, God having become *flesh*, is what saves."

According to Irenaeus, not to mention Christianity, truth has been decisively revealed in the flesh of Jesus Christ. After all, Jesus never said, "And now what you have all been waiting for—the secret message of truth." He said, "I am . . . the truth" (John 14:6). In keeping with this logic of incarnation, Irenaeus is more or less saying that no one gospel has the bottom line on the person of Jesus

Christ. Each evangelist writes a truthful account so far as a fac-
tual account of Jesus' life goes. And each evangelist offers a self-con-
tained account that stands on its own two feet, and each gospel can
be used, if properly read, to refute various heresies. But no one
gospel gives an exhaustive account of Jesus Christ.

Comparing the Gospels to the pillars that held up the tabernacle
of Israel, that is, the mobile temple-tent of God before Solomon's
temple was built, Irenaeus argues that the four gospels give four
perspectives to the truth. No one gospel is coextensive with the
truth of Jesus Christ himself. Together the four gospels create the
framework for the truth and mark off its boundaries; the truth, the
essence of the gospel, lies in the space between four gospels.

Corresponding to the complexity of Christ's person, and the
inability of any one gospel to comprehend the manifold wonders of
Christ, is the diversity of humanity itself. There must be four
gospels, Irenaeus says, because there are four corners to the world.
Here the bishop of Lyons is thinking of Revelation 7:1–2. It is a passage dealing with the ingathering of believers from all over the
world. Irenaeus is reflecting on the question of the plurality of the
Gospels and the nature of Christian mission. His point seems to be
that just as there is a manifold richness to Christ, the true human,
there is also a rich diversity to humanity. The story of Jesus needs to
be told in four ways in order to convey the diversity of Christ to a
correspondingly diverse humanity needing to hear the story. The
problem with the Gnostic notion, that salvation comes from the
knowledge of an idea, is that ideas are inextricably culturally bound,
even if they refuse to admit as much. Marx saw salvation in the
proletariat's overcoming of capitalism. The German philosopher
Hegel saw salvation as the outworking of Spirit in human existence.

The Enlightenment saw salvation in education and progress. But Marxism, Hegelianism, and the Enlightenment are all working from an idea that privileges certain cultural assumptions. They all pretend to offer a transcendent philosophy, but they are all equally provincial. And each movement, so totalizing and so convinced of the transcendent status of its philosophy, seeks to have its way with an unsuspecting world.

Reviewing Ehrman's remarks quoted at the beginning of this chapter concerning those who are quick to meld together the four gospels, I think his point is well taken. Modern-day Christians seem to have a curious discomfiture with the fact that we have four gospels instead of just one. When you have four gospels, it is felt, you have four different portraits of Christ, and this raises the possibility that one or more of these portraits might say different things ("Oh my!"). Well, the truth is we do have four gospels and they do say four different things. And when it comes to reading each of the gospels, we must let each evangelist speak on his own terms. There is certainly a sense in which Ehrman is quite right: somehow we feel that in order to salvage the message of Mark, we have to send Matthew in for the rescue. And when Luke doesn't seem quite right, Mark is always there to lend a helping hand to tell us what Jesus really meant. Or when Luke 6:20 has Jesus saying, "Blessed are you poor," someone might be quick to volunteer, "Yes, that may be, but Matthew 5:3 reads, 'Blessed are the poor in spirit,' all of which means that Luke really meant to say what Matthew says." But this is as unhelpful as it is inappropriate. Luke clearly says, "Blessed are you poor." Luke's Jesus has to be understood for what he has to say without Matthew's Jesus interrupting. The problem with sending one evangelist in to rescue another is that this becomes an easy way to get the Gospels to say what we want to hear. (Why is it that evangelicals always tend to interpret Luke 6:20 in light of Matthew 5:3 and not vice versa?) To me, this is just manipulating the Gospels as a magician might manipulate a stack of cards. Now you see Luke's message—now you don't.

However, as with many things in life, when it comes to appreciating the diversity of the Gospels, we have to walk a fine line. We must avoid two extremes. One extreme is to neglect each evangelist's unique contribution; the other extreme is to assume that the uniqueness of each of the four stories cancels out any consonance, theological or historical, among the four gospels. Ehrman is loud and clear in warning us against falling off of the first side. But the other side is to forget Irenaeus's point that the four gospels speak together and testify together in concert to the diversity of Christ and humanity. The reason Ehrman fails to speak to this danger is that he doesn't seem to believe that there is a concert. But this judgment in turn is informed by certain historical and theological presuppositions.

In chapter seven, I argued that the veracity of the evangelists depends in large measure on their relationship to the events they recount. For example, Luke claimed that his sources included oral and written accounts of those who had personal contact with the likes of Jesus and the twelve disciples. Lacking any convincing reason to mistrust this claim, we must envisage Luke using Mark as one of a number of sources. Luke relied on Mark sometimes heavily, sometimes rather lightly.

But if, as Ehrman sees it, Luke only had Mark to depend on in retelling those stories that also occur in Mark, then this has certain consequences for how we look at Luke's activity. In the scenario envisaged by Ehrman, Luke might as well have been holed up in a room somewhere with a blank papyrus before him, a pen in hand, and a copy of Mark at his side. He then sets himself to changing Mark because he wants to improve upon Mark. His changes are not just reinterpretations; they are challenges to Mark's ability as a Jesus storyteller. Ehrman's Luke is not setting up his gospel alongside of Mark's; this Luke is hoping to supplant and replace Mark. At bottom, Luke's approach to Mark is entirely outside of any sense of community; his stance is adversarial. The final authority on Jesus is the one who gets in the final word.

When you think about New Testament scholars and what—in addition to teaching and committee work—they do for a living, you find a curious parallel. When you think of someone secluded away in a study, someone with a word processor at his fingertips, someone who has a book or set of books whose thrust needs to be challenged or revised, you're thinking of a New Testament scholar. Is it going too far in saying that countless New Testament scholars, not just Ehrman, read themselves into the shoes of the gospel writers? I think not. One of the most important differences between Luke-according-to-Ehrman and the historical Luke is that the latter was no lone wolf but belonged to a community that recognized the authority of those who told Jesus stories. In writing his gospel, Luke was adding his gospel to the mix, not necessarily supplanting earlier endeavors.

I argued in chapter 6 that the gospel writers wrote what they did under the auspices of the apostolic community. They wrote as ones who were self-consciously advancing the story and words of Jesus in an authoritative way. The stories they wrote were not merely haphazard remembrances; they were records that were to serve as the basis of Christian proclamation and mission. By composing these gospels, the evangelists saw themselves as fulfilling their role as the continuation of both the true community of God and the true temple.

In this respect the evangelists, and indeed all the New Testament writers, were in a class by themselves. There would be many Christian writings that would be produced and promulgated down through the centuries; such writings continue to be written today. But if the apostles truly believed that Jesus was the Messiah and that Israel's hopes lay in his ongoing movement even after his death and resurrection (indeed precisely because of his death and resurrection), then they also likely saw themselves as having the select role of reflecting on that revelatory event. Since the apostles constituted the basis of the new temple, and this new temple required new revelation, it only made sense that the apostles viewed themselves as conduits of that revelation.

All this has implications for how we understand the interrelationship of the Gospels. If Mark was among the first gospels to be written, then the latter evangelists ascribed to his text some degree of authority. Presumably then when they wrote their gospels, they wrote with a view not of replacing Mark but of supplementing him. This means that Mark provided the context against which the other gospels sought to be understood. In this sense, if we wish to take the Gospels on their own terms, we *do* have to understand them against one another. If this leads to creating a virtual kind of metagospel, a mental reconstruction of what actually happened in the life of Jesus, then so be it. But the fact that God saw fit to give us four gospels, not one, means that any metagospel we come up with, any vision of the historical Jesus, must be subsidiary to the individual witnesses of the four gospels. Behind the four gospels there is one gospel of our historical imagination, but this should not overshadow the fact that the one gospel has been made known in four accounts.

While I certainly would not want to agree with everything Irenaeus has to say, I think his point about the four gospels is something that needs to be recovered for Christians today. I certainly could have used a dose of Irenaeus while I sat there in Mr. Mac's class slowly pawing the carpet with my foot as I wondered about blind men and elephants.

All the world religions, we were told, were like a group of blind men groping their way about different parts of one and the same elephant. Despite the limitations of this illustration—particularly the assumptions it makes, including the grandiose assumption that we Western, Enlightenment folk are the only ones who have the eyes and positioning to see the whole elephant (see chapter 4)—it has a certain degree of persuasiveness to it. It speaks to our intuition that God, if he is truly God, exceeds our ability to grasp him. When it comes to knowing God, our sense is that we are blind beggars feeling our way around the edges.

Christians need to be careful how they preach the gospel. They need to be careful as to how they speak about Jesus Christ, his person and words. I have been arguing that, historically speaking, we can have a fair deal of confidence that the Gospels give us the words—not to mention the life—of Jesus. But this confidence does not mean that we have fully grasped Jesus, that we have intellectually mastered him, that he is in our back pocket. Over the course of history, when people come to think of Jesus in this way, he suddenly becomes demoted to being an accoutrement for another social, political, or intellectual program altogether. Beware of people who give you the impression that they have Jesus completely figured out. The living Jesus refuses to fit neatly into *anyone's* back pocket.

The fact that there are four gospels rather than one means that Jesus cannot be reduced—as the Gnostics would want to have it—to a datum, a system, or an idea. In bringing light to darkness, God sent a life that was to be a light for all people. The light is so brilliant that no one window pane was enough to contain its glory. Usually, in order to convey an idea you only need one perspective; God needed four perspectives. And we, like people being slowly healed from our blindness, are slowly feeling our way around the elephantine love of Jesus. One day we will see fully, but now we content ourselves with experiencing Jesus as those partially blind. The four gospels guide us to Jesus, plant our hands on one of his four sides, and say, "For now, until you see him face-to-face, you have us as your guides. Listen to each one of us. Listen to all of us. For now, that is as close as you will come to capturing the words of Jesus."

NINE

MISTAKING MATTERS

That is to say, once a scribe changes a text—whether accidentally or intentionally—then those changes are *permanent* in his manuscript (unless, of course, another scribe comes along to correct the mistake). The next scribe who copies *that* manuscript copies those mistakes (thinking they are what the text said), and he adds mistakes of his own. The next scribe who then copies *that* manuscript copies the mistakes of both his predecessors and adds mistakes of his own, and so on. . . . Mistakes multiply and get repeated; sometimes they get corrected and sometimes they get compounded. And so it goes. For centuries.

—BART EHRMAN, *Misquoting Jesus*

One weekend not too long ago, I was staying at a hotel in Washington DC that was situated across the street from a park space that doubled as a venue for public events. As was obvious from the prominent sign and big top, the Cirque du Soleil was in town. The Cirque du Soleil is one of the world's most famous circuses. Its performers are supposed to be among the best at what they do. Walking along 14th Street, I could hear the cheering of the crowd from under the big top.

My mind raced back to the last time I was at the circus, years ago as a child. I thought about seeing the trapeze act and how the next day at the school playground I was inspired to swing from the monkey bars as if I, too, simply at will, could fly through the air with the greatest of ease. Of course, I could not. Even if I had all the equipment available to a real trapezist, I could not. The best I could do at the time was simply hang there for a few seconds then fall to the ground. One of the great things about being a kid is that you can always at least pretend to be a circus trapezist or the next Michael Jordan without having to take seriously the fact that those who approach perfection do so because they have given their lives to it.

No one can attain to the trapezist's level of gymnastic agility and precision overnight. In addition to the right mix of DNA, it takes countless hours of hands-on training, both on an individual basis and in the company of those who have gone before. It has to be this way. When you're passing spinning, airborne bodies from one pair of hands to another, there's not much room for error. Minor glitches—things that only a few insiders would notice—might not constitute the proverbial "show stopper." But should a major mistake occur, should someone get dropped in transmission, everybody under the big top knows about it soon enough. I have to imagine that when mistakes do occur, big or small, somebody makes it his or her business to sit down afterward and figure out what went wrong.

In the world of New Testament studies, there is a discipline that makes a business out of determining the origin of errors in the manuscript tradition: textual criticism. The goal of textual criticism is to locate even the most minor differences between surviving manuscripts, develop theories as to how those differences/errors got there, and work toward recovering the original wording of the twenty-seven (or so) autograph texts that stand behind our New Testament canon.[1] No text critic would venture to claim that we have successfully reconstructed the New Testament word for word. But after centuries of collecting, sorting, and comparing manuscripts, many would say that we have come pretty darn close. And as discussion continues and new manuscripts come to light, I believe we get closer and closer, even as, paradoxically, we are moving farther and farther from the events surrounding the writing of the Gospels.

To repeat a statement made earlier in this book: Jesus Christ has revealed himself once and for all, and this revelation has been recorded once and for all. But the singularity of the Christ-event apparently did not exempt the church from having to spend two thousand years (and still counting) both grappling with the theological significance of Christ's coming and refining its historical understanding of that moment. The art of getting back to the very first texts, textual criticism, is just one more way of shedding a more precise light on how that moment was first recorded.

It bears stating that whereas textual criticism as an academic discipline is a modern development, text criticism itself is not. Under the big top of the church, text criticism has been practiced for almost as long as Christianity has been in existence. This is borne out not only by the example of such prominent figures as Jerome (347–420), who sought out the best texts in the original language before preparing his translation of the now-famous Latin Vulgate, but also by lesser lights who can be heard to complain about the circulation of error-laden manuscripts. Obviously, if the early Christians didn't care about errors, they would not have sought to establish the authentic text. Neither would they have complained about those who miscopied the text. A project like Jerome's and the expressed longing for uncorrupted copies of Scripture indicate that even near the dawn of the church age there were those who took it upon themselves to identify errors and remedy errant manuscripts. Even if pre–printing press Christians have not always had the tools or the databases that we have today, they have always been committed to textual criticism of sorts. They have been so because they wanted to ensure that the message from and about Jesus was not lost in transmission.

This is an important point because the book under review here has a way of giving the impression that it wasn't until the time of Erasmus (1466–1536) that people began to care about recovering the original Greek manuscript. To be sure, in medieval western Europe (where until the High Middle Ages, Latin had all but eclipsed the language of the New Testament), informal and ad hoc attempts to clean up the text were frustrated by the scribes' relative ignorance of Greek. But the textual tradition in the eastern half of the empire retained a widespread ability and interest in accurately preserving the Greek text. The deeply conservative outlook of the medieval period, characterized broadly by its placing a premium on the *auctoritas* (authority) of the ancients, also suggests that whatever mishaps befell the text of the New Testament, there remained an abiding concern to avoid errors and safeguard the original traditions of the past.

This resolve traces itself right down to the beginnings of Christianity. In an earlier chapter, I argued that the Jesus movement took shape in a decidedly Jewish context, a point on which Ehrman agrees.[2] When we consider best Jewish practices in preserving the Hebrew Old Testament text, we see that the scribes must have taken painstaking measures to check the accuracy of their copies.[3] Because the ancient Jews held the Scriptures in such high regard and copied their sacred texts with scrupulous care, we can assume that those Jewish Christians who first copied the words of Jesus did so with the same fear and trembling. While it may be true, as Ehrman points out, that many of the first copyists of New Testament texts were not professional scribes, this possibility hardly drives us to despair.[4] Given the Jewish-style reverence for authoritative texts among the first Christians, the copyist's religious commitment to properly preserving the written tradition may well have

134

offset the disadvantages of failing to employ someone who copied texts for a living. We must suppose, after all, that a Christian who took it upon himself or herself to make an unprofessional copy was primarily interested in getting it done right. The contracted scribe was primarily interested in getting paid and getting it done.

Even when toward the close of the first century Christianity began to sever its ties with Judaism and Jewish culture, Christians did not suddenly cease to be a people of the book. The Old Testament together with the New Testament underwrote everything Christians believed and practiced. So while we would not want to romanticize the laborious process of copying down long texts for long hours, we also would not want to make the opposite mistake of thinking that the scribes were coldly indifferent to the significance of their task, as if they might as well have been reproducing pages from a phone book or π to the 50,000th decimal place. From the second century down to the invention of the printing press, the vast majority of those who transmitted biblical manuscripts believed that they were copying the very words of God.

The confessional (faith-based) setting of textual transmission, I believe, has two notable implications. In the first place, the Christian scribal tradition, contrary to Ehrman's claims, did not see its task as including the reinterpretation and rewriting of biblical text. For those in this tradition, the Bible was the sacred page (*sacra pagina*), the imprint of God himself on the vellum or papyrus sheet. The words of Scripture were words that the ancient and medieval Christians knew well—far better than Christians today know their Bibles. As people of the book, the scribes (especially those in the monasteries) ate, drank, slept, and breathed Scripture. They memorized Scripture; they kept it in their hearts. Scribes almost certainly interpreted the master text and emended it as necessary, but it was not their standard practice—as Ehrman states it—to put "the text in their own words rather than in the words of the original authors."[5] Given their reverence for Scripture, the last thing on their minds was to change it.

According to Ehrman, it should come as no surprise that scribes behind the New Testament manuscripts made substantive alterations. After all, Matthew and Luke had no qualms about changing *their* master text. The scribes may have changed the text "*less* radically" than the gospel writers, but "change it they did, sometimes accidentally, sometimes intentionally."[6] For Ehrman, the comparison between the gospel writers and those who later recopied the gospel texts boils down to a difference of degree (that is, the number of changes they were willing to make on the text), not a difference of kind (how they saw their role).

However, this analogy between the scribes' altering of texts and the gospel writers' reworking of Mark is convincing only if the two activities (copying a gospel and writing one) are assumed to be roughly equivalent undertakings. In other words, if Matthew and Luke saw themselves as the earliest of Christian scribes and as little more, or if the Christian copyists of the Roman era or Middle Ages saw themselves as being on par with the gospel writers themselves, then this may be a valid argument. But either one of these points is extremely difficult to make stick. The gospel writers were not simply reworking one another's material, nor were they merely giving their own slant on the history of Jesus. Rather, the evangelists saw themselves as being conduits of revelation, as having the unique task of laying out the story of Jesus in order that it might serve as an authoritative norm for the church community. If Luke told a different story than Mark, it is, again, not because he hopes to replace Mark but because he is supplementing Mark's authoritative account with an equally authoritative account. We have no grounds for imagining that the gospel writers considered themselves to be mere scribes of a prior tradition; nor have we grounds for believing that the scribes claimed equal footing with the likes of Matthew or Luke. Although Ehrman wishes to level the playing field between gospel writer and copyist, the radically different ways in which they envisaged their respective tasks makes his analogy entirely unhelpful. Writing as an authoritative voice, Luke was convinced he had the God-given right to tell a story different from that of Mark: no Christian scribe of the succeeding centuries would dare to make such a claim. The scribe's job—he knew full well—was to get Luke down right.

A second implication of the fact that the New Testament was handed down in a confessional context is that the copyists were not just copyists but also self-involved readers. For some, the inability of the scribes to serve as disinterested and objective transmitters may stand to compromise their ability to pass along the text faithfully. This is part of Ehrman's point when he shows that a scribe's orthodox commitments can sometimes have a harmful effect on the accurate transmission of Scripture.[7] But despite the occasional indiscretions of an overzealous scribe, I would argue just the opposite: that, generally speaking, the religious commitment of those handing down the text would have been more of a help than a hindrance in conserving it. For just as the best discerners of errors at the circus are the circus performers themselves, those for whom the routine has become second nature, so, too, those who are most likely to detect errors in the transmission of the New Testament are those who live in the Scriptures.

This is not to say that those scribes *must* know their scriptures if they are to have any chance of rooting out errors either in the master text or in their own copy. Most mistakes people make in copying are quite noticeable even to someone who is relatively unfamiliar with the master text or subject matter. Think back, for example, to the fifth grade when you wrote out the final draft of your big report on Native Americans. When you turned it in, you were confident that it was one of the best in the class. Then when you got it back, you saw that it was covered with red ink. Here you forgot to append a period, there you misspelled the word "Iroquois," over here you simply dropped a word altogether. None of these mistakes were in the first draft, and all of them were easy enough to make. But it is usually the case that the easiest mistakes to make are also the easiest ones to spot, then to fix. Even if your fifth-grade teacher doesn't know squat about the Iroquois, she still can spill a cartridge of red ink on your paper because she can gather what you *meant* to say. Because oral and written communication involve an agreed-upon system (sentences need periods, prepositional phrases need a preposition, etc.), disruptions to that system draw attention to themselves very quickly. Certainly, errors can and will creep into any hand copying of texts. But the preponderance of such errors are easily detected and corrected.

All the same, when it comes to preserving the Gospels and the rest of the New Testament documents, these sacred texts have a distinct advantage over your fifth-grade report on Native Americans. This advantage, again, has to do with the fact that they have been preserved in the context of a faith community. The New Testament texts are not just a pack of stories and letters; they are a collection that became the building blocks of Christian belief. That means, in addition to whatever narrative and grammatical logic the documents might have, a logic that usually penalizes itself once violated, the community of Christian believers also saw these texts as yielding up their own theological logic. Down through the ages, those who have copied these texts have held specific beliefs about the nature of God and humanity, about Jesus Christ and salvation, and about the church and the end of history. Of course, there was in the early church—as continues to be the case today—an ample difference of opinion on a number of secondary matters, but in a short time the church as it interpreted Scripture began to achieve a consensus on some pretty big questions. Once this consensus started taking shape, it was natural for the early church to use its accepted positions as an interpretive grid for resolving places where Scripture's meaning was less clear. Writing in the late second century, Irenaeus calls this emerging consensus the "rule of faith." We might also call this the tradition of the Great Church; after the Council of Nicea (AD 325), we call it "orthodoxy."

To be clear, I am not arguing that the only ones who copied Scripture held to a position comparable to Nicean orthodoxy. In fact, as far as we know, the first commentator on the gospel of John (which he presumably copied in his commentary) was anything but orthodox.[8] But the eventual dominance of orthodoxy in the second century meant the establishment of a particular convictional framework that for orthodox Christians everywhere made sense of the individual data of Scripture. It will not do, then, to imagine the transmission of Scripture apart from a shared communal life and a shared understanding as to what Scripture meant. Of course, once we realize that most texts were reproduced for a larger purpose than an individual's private and personal use, then we must also recognize that these reproductions of the master text were inevitably constrained and regulated by the community's interpretation, understanding, and recollection of Scripture.

Because Ehrman does not believe that the early church had a shared understanding as to what Scripture meant and, therefore, had no true communal life (since it lacked a unified belief), he unavoidably overstates the isolated nature of transmission as well as the frequency and compounding of error in the manuscript tradition. But even if Western religion today is, sadly, a kind of every-man-for-himself affair, we should not superimpose our radical individualism, along with our current state of interpretive free-for-all ("My interpretation is just as valid as your interpretation"), back on the early church's transmission of Scripture. It is true, at least if Irenaeus is right, that Gnostic believers trafficked in "various systems of truth," but to the extent that those systems depended on the details of the received text, this dependence would induce Gnostic scribes to be careful in preserving those details for their Gnostic communities.[9] Established traditions of interpretation—orthodox, Gnostic, or other—have a way of making texts resistant to change.

If the original text of the New Testament can be compared to a plush lawn of grass and textual corruptions to weeds, then I am saying that the hired gardeners (the scribes down through the ages) have generally been quick to identify and eradicate weeds. The gardeners have been aware that the family who owns the property is deeply interested in preserving the lawn; the gardeners also have been well aware of what the grass should look like in most places so that when they encounter something that isn't grass, they pick up on it. Granted, sometimes the gardener himself planted a weed (in the hopes of its choking out what he perceived, rightly or wrongly, to be an even more pernicious weed). But we must imagine that it was far more common for the gardener to recall what the lawn should look like in that part of the yard and do the necessary uprooting and replanting. If the original lawn remained healthy and relatively weed-free long enough for the first gardeners to acquaint themselves thoroughly with the grass, then under this kind of care it would seem to be rather difficult, but of course not impossible, for weeds to take root.

But what if the original lawn did not stay healthy for very long? What if the first generation of gardeners inherited a big mix of Kentucky bluegrass and crabgrass and could not always tell the difference as to which belonged and which did not? Some scholars believe that this is precisely the case. What we really have, they say, is not a lawn with a few weeds, but a lawn that has experienced cross-pollination from just about every weed-infested lawn in the subdivision—all resulting in a mishmash of bluegrass, crabgrass, dandelion, chickweed, and spurge. In other words, we should give up talking about the "original text" altogether. As one writer argues, just as we have, for many years now, lost all hope of identifying the "original text" of many Shakespearean plays, it's high time we dispensed with talking about the "original text" of the New Testament.[10]

One reason for surmising that the original lawn was overrun by weeds at such an early date, that is, before the gardeners even showed up, has to do with the observation that when the church fathers quoted the New Testament, their citations often differed considerably from what we find in our so-called stronger witnesses. It is reasoned that if Justin Martyr or Irenaeus did not stick very closely to the wording of the received text (as we understand it), then maybe this received text was not established as the standard until some time *after* the second century. But in my view, the second-century writer's loosely worded recall of Scripture provides little evidence for an unstable second-century text. Today pastors and laypeople alike constantly paraphrase and harmonize Scripture without thinking twice. They do so not because the text of their Bible is unstable, but because they know that sometimes there is rhetorical benefit in reshaping their citation according to the context. Who is to say that people like Irenaeus did not feel the same freedom? Using the church fathers as evidence in textual criticism is a shaky procedure, fraught with its own set of difficulties.[11]

Against this rather skeptical position, a good number of textual critics feel not only that it makes sense to talk about the original New Testament text (there is a plush lawn out there somewhere despite the weeds), but also that this text *is* largely recoverable. Their confidence is well grounded. After all, we have roughly 5,500 manuscript witnesses to the New Testament. There is no other book and no other set of books that can even come close to comparing with this level of attestation. Compared to classicists who study non-Christian Greek and Latin texts (which are lucky if they can show a dozen manuscripts to their name), New Testament scholars can boast an embarrassment of riches.[12] I would argue that with such excellent evidence in hand and the application of well-reasoned procedures, textual criticism not only can, but already has, come very close to reconstructing the text as it first came to light through the hand of Matthew, Mark, Luke, John, and the rest. The centuries that modern text critics (today's scribes and gardeners) have spent on their hands and knees poring over manuscripts, that is, sorting out the grass from the weeds, has been time well spent.

But this is not, it seems, what Ehrman wants us to believe. Instead, much like Nietzsche, who regarded recorded history as a collage of errors perpetuated by those who would profit from receiving those errors as truth, our author repeatedly sounds the alarm that we must not sacrifice truth on the altar of Christian orthodoxy; we must not be willfully naïve to the fact that the New Testament has been utterly corrupted by copyists' mistakes. "Imagine all the people," Ehrman seems to say, "copying down the New Testament texts through the centuries. Now imagine all their errors!" In effect, what Nietzsche was saying about God, Ehrman is now saying about the Bible: the text of the New Testament is dead, and Christians have killed it with their own pens. This is the heart of Ehrman's thesis.

But strangely, despite Ehrman's insistence on utter corruption of our text, he dedicates considerable space in his book toward proving that the actual autograph actually said this or that—generally against the received reading. As far as logic of argumentation goes, this is one of the most disconcerting aspects of the book. In one moment, our author seems to be saying, "Due to the proliferating weeds of scribal errors and tampering, we can't know what the original plush lawn looked like." In the next moment, when it suits his case, he goes on to say, "Now let me tell you what the green grass of the autograph looks like here, and why what most of you think of as weed is actually grass." "Well," the puzzled reader has a right to ask, "can we get back to the verdant pasture of the original or not?" Ehrman needs to know that you can't have it both ways.

Not only does Ehrman exaggerate the frequency of textual corruption in our received text; he is equally given to overstatement, even sensationalism, when it comes to deliberating on what is at stake. Again, to be sure, there are a number of points in our Greek Bibles at which we cannot be sure of the original's precise wording. But I submit that the doctrinal stakes riding on those points are, despite Ehrman's insistence to the contrary, less than earthshaking. Ehrman argues that Mark's Jesus was angry before he healed the paralytic, not filled with compassion. He argues that Luke's Jesus had it all under control in Gethsemane and did not experience the emotional torment that a later scribe attributed to him. Even if Ehrman were making a convincing case on these two points (I think he does on the latter point but not the former), this does not tell us anything about Jesus that could not already be gathered from other places in the Gospels.

In this case the proverb is true: you can't tell a book by its cover. The title of *Misquoting Jesus*, not to mention the jacket summary, promises far more than it delivers. When we view this book in the light of day, we find nothing in it that makes for breaking news, nothing in it that demands that we revamp our understanding of the early church or Jesus. And, to boot, not once are we shown a place where Jesus himself is misquoted. When we consider the gospel of Mark (leaving aside the longer ending), we see that less than 1 percent of Jesus' words are subject to any serious question at all. But in no case does this dispute measurably affect the meaning of Jesus' statements.[13] If this is misquoting, then you would be hard-pressed to find *any* article in *any* newspaper on *any* given day that doesn't "misquote" its sources. Did the scribes really "misquote" Jesus? I think not.

The Jesus whom the first-century Christians met in the four gospels two thousand years ago is the very same Jesus we meet in our Bibles today. If there are minor discrepancies between the wordings of the gospel manuscripts, this does not invalidate Christian faith. On the contrary, it reminds us that perfect truth and perfect beauty, that which demands our worship, is not to be equated with the Bible, but with the one to whom the Bible witnesses. Over the centuries the church has received God incarnate through the sometimes faltering hands of the scribes, and Jesus has been successfully passed along without being lost in transmission. This transmission is not perfect, but it is adequate. Ehrman and the Enlightenment demand what is perfect, but the God of perfect gifts demands a response from what is adequate.

TEN

MISLEADING PENS

Why didn't these other groups simply read their New Testaments to see that their views were wrong? It is because there *was* no New Testament. To be sure, all the books of the New Testament had been written by this time, but there were lots of other books as well, also claiming to be Jesus's own apostles—other gospels, acts, epistles and apocalypses having very different perspectives from those found in the books that eventually came to be called the New Testament. . . . During the second and third centuries . . . there was no agreed-upon canon—and no agreed-upon theology.

—BART EHRMAN, *Misquoting Jesus*

But when, really," he asked, "did the church canonize the New Testament?"

In the midst of a class lecture on the consolidation of proto-orthodoxy (orthodoxy before AD 325), I paused to look at my questioner. He was a young man with a beard, long dirty-blond hair, a tall forehead, and a serene gaze: he looked like the spitting image of Jesus, at least as he has been popularly represented. I had to pause because I knew his question was entirely serious and that, given his background, no one-minute answer would do.

With my permission, the young man had been invited by his slightly older brother to sit in on a few classes. The brothers, by their own words, had been raised together in a "fundamentalist household." A wholesome upbringing, they said, but lots of rules without much explanation for those rules. As the older brother entered into adulthood, his theology changed and he came to prefer the label "evangelical" to "fundamentalist." Around the same time, his slightly younger brother also made some changes in his thinking, but in a very different direction. When people asked him his religious affiliation, he would simply say, "Gnostic." He wasn't joking. This Jesus look-alike belonged, so he said, to one of only a handful of active Gnostic churches in the Northeast.

When you are teaching about the first two centuries of Christianity, you cannot help but spend considerable time on the prolonged battle between the proto-orthodox camp and their archrivals, the Gnostics. As you might imagine, it certainly changes how you teach this subject the day you realize that Gnosticism, far from being a relic of ancient history, has found living and breathing representation in your very classroom. It also changes things when you've always sensed that Gnosticism never really completely died out, but went underground only to surface later in various manifestations. The battle between orthodoxy and Gnosticism isn't over yet and probably won't be any time soon.

As far as my young Gnostic friend was concerned, I was aware of what he was being told by his church. Original Christian belief, they told him, was actually incredibly diverse, and it was only an ancient, proto-fundamentalist conspiracy to rewrite the past that made it look as though everybody always believed the same thing. This claim, a common one in current scholarship and one to which Ehrman subscribes, is subject to criticism in that it is simply replacing one oversimplification (all followers of Jesus believed the same thing) with another one (no followers of Jesus believed the same thing).[1] Conspiracy theories have a way of resonating with our postmodern culture (thanks to the hermeneutic of suspicion left to us by Marx, Nietzsche, and Freud). But even conspiracy theories must make peace with the facts.

After graduating from high school, I took a summer job in New York City with a major international grain-trading firm. On weekdays I would ride the underground train from New Jersey into the bowels of the World Trade Center, walk over to Chase Manhattan Plaza, then from there spend the day hitting the pavement as a street messenger. Sometimes on the way back from a delivery I would stop to buy a Coke or a kebab. And sometimes I would stop and listen to the Jews for Jesus, who periodically congregated near the corner of Wall and Broad streets. With their white cotton button-down shirts, rolled-up sleeves, and armpits soaked with perspiration, they preached that the Messiah had already come in Jesus. Sometimes this provoked heated debate with other-minded Jews as they passed by. It could be quite a scene. If I had a few minutes to spare, I would stop and listen, for I could hardly resist "a scene." Besides, I was not yet done with Jesus, nor was he done with me.

My messenger job had been lined up through my father, who was a physician for Mr. Klein, the president of the North American division. Aside from our initial meeting when he offered me the job, I didn't see Mr. Klein much. Once in a while he would duck into the dispatch office. But he certainly had more important things to do than to check in on one of the messenger boys. Not that there was much to check in on. When "business" was slow, we messengers (a mix of college-age and retirement-age men) sat and read. Most of the guys read the *New York Daily News* multiple times over; I was usually reading Nietzsche or Thomas Mann. Not that I really understood Mann or Nietzsche even after all that time of reading them (I still don't), but I fancied myself a young intellectual and such authors were, therefore, required reading.

At the end of one workday, Mr. Klein spotted me at a distance in the hallway. "Hey," he said, "would you like a ride home?" I was taken aback at the offer and felt slightly uncomfortable at the thought. After all, though the commute home in a sweaty train was no fun, my typical routine would not take nearly as much emotional energy as would going home with my great-great-grand-boss. I didn't know if I was up to it.

"Well, no, I shouldn't," I said.

"Aw, c'mon," he said.

And with his added insistence I realized that as weird as it would be for me to commute home with Mr. Klein, it would be weirder to keep turning him down. So I agreed. He told me to meet him at his car on the street. When I did, he was already in the backseat of his limousine, and the driver was standing there outside of the car waiting for me. As I drew near, the driver opened the rear door; I ducked in, and the door closed behind me. As I was getting settled, I thought to myself, *Maybe I can handle this after all.* We were on our way.

After Mr. Klein and I exchanged some brief chitchat, he told me that he had some work to do and popped open his briefcase. I had my work too—reading work. That day I had packed a paperback called *Subliminal Seduction.* When Mr. Klein interrupted himself and asked me what I was reading, I probably gave him more than he was asking for. "Oh, it's a book about the advertising industry," I told him, "and all the ways in which they use sexual images on a subconscious level to win the consumer over. It's awful, really. It's like brainwashing." From there I proceeded to launch into my speech about no matter how bad Madison Avenue was, Wall Street was worse. It was shameless the way these big corporations profiteered off the backs of the poor. Of course Mr. Klein listened, smiled, and nodded appropriately, all very graciously. It never occurred to me in the midst of this speech, lasting at least the length of the Holland Tunnel, that my audience happened to be the president of one such "big corporation." Nor did it occur to me, as the limo pulled into my family's driveway in Summit, New Jersey, and as the driver jumped out to get my door (hopefully for as many friends and family as possible to see), that I was, after all, enjoying certain benefits from at least one of these corporations.

Not that I now believe that I was *all* wrong back then. But I wasn't all right either. Obviously, as anyone living in post-Enron America knows, big corporations can be devastatingly corrupt. But big business does not have the corner on the greed-and-lust-for-power market. Certainly, such institutions may have much more latitude for exercising that greed, which is a problem in its own right, but that doesn't make all other institutions or any one person less greedy by nature. George Orwell tells us that power corrupts and that absolute power corrupts absolutely. But I think Orwell is mistaken. Power is merely the catalyst that allows the germinating seed of corruption, already embedded within humanity, to sprout to the surface, while absolute power brings the same bitter shoot to full blossom. This is not just my idea. When Jesus talks about the human condition, he assumes our evil nature as a matter of course (Matt. 7:11; Mark 7:20–23; et al.).

But if you're not prepared to take Jesus' word for it and have already discarded the notion that "all humans are essentially good," you need somewhere to pin the blame. You need, in other words, a genealogy of evil. My strategy as an eighteen-year-old, a common one, was to think that all of society's ills could be traced to a conspiracy among a small cadre of powerful elites. Surely, when things go wrong, your best bet is to imagine a story that begins with a smoke-filled room where bald, overweight, middle-aged men in dark suits rub their hands together in connivance amid the sound of hearty laughter. Whatever their machinations, whatever their pronouncements and policies, justice demands that we unmask such abuses of power for what they are.

While I'm sure many bad institutional practices do trace themselves back to a scene much like this, problems arise when this narrative is instinctively trotted out as an explanatory tool that, like cheap merchandise sold on late-night television, "can do it all." Often, when you take a look for yourself, you see that such a tool, far from slicing and dicing alternative explanations, in reality just doesn't cut much of anything at all. When Ehrman writes that there was "no agreed-upon theology" and no canon in the second century, he is appealing to a well-worn conspiracy theory. It is a theory that holds that there were actually more than a few dozen gospels in circulation—all of them on par with Matthew, Mark, Luke, and John—until some elitist powerbrokers, not least the old and crotchety figure of Irenaeus, put the kibosh on such diversity and restricted the church to four gospels and no more. Ehrman belongs to a line of scholarship that believes that it was Irenaeus who invented the fourfold gospel canon; he did so in order to take control of a chaotic church and rule out alternative sources of revelation.

Irenaeus was the first to mention all four by name and give a justification for there being four.[2] Yet for many scholars, including myself, Irenaeus was not the first to propound four (and only four) gospels. Rather, his argument smacks of the sense that he is simply reinforcing a notion already well accepted by his readers. The Muratorian canon, a list of authoritative writings that leads us to believe that there were four and only four gospels, may well predate Irenaeus by a decade or two. A close reading of the still-earlier figure Justin Martyr also yields the conclusion that there were four "memoirs" of the apostles being used in Christian worship in the mid-second century. The author of the longer ending of Mark (datable to ca. AD 125) seems to have had a fourfold gospel handy, as perhaps was true of Papias as well.[3]

Besides this, it should be mentioned that some of our earliest hard manuscript evidence also demonstrates the liturgical use of a four-gospel codex right around the time of Irenaeus. If Ehrman and Pagels are right, then within a few years of Irenaeus's passing remarks regarding the four gospels, the worldwide church dropped its own traditions and immediately toed the line. But Irenaeus was the bishop of Lyons, not the bishop of the universal church. When Irenaeus said, "Jump!" the rest of the Christian world did *not* say, "How high?" At least we have no evidence to that effect.

Therefore, a much more than reasonable case can be made that Irenaeus did not invent the fourfold canon but merely inherited it. And because there is no historical indication that the second-century church was structured in a way that made such a top-down decision even possible, the elitist conspiracy theory here simply runs aground. The fourfold gospel was explicitly deemed authoritative by the end of the second century not because any ecclesiastical muckety-mucks said so but because the four gospels had always had a de facto authority ("Using the four gospels is the way we've always done it") within the church. Presumably, the four gospels originally had this status because of alleged ties to the apostles, who, as I have argued, were granted the role of succeeding Jesus in his temple movement.

But this leaves one question unanswered: what about those "lots of other books" that were claimed to have been written by "Jesus's own apostles—other gospels, acts, epistles and apocalypses"? What about the *Gospel of Judas*, the *Gospel of Thomas*, and the *Gospel of Philip*—to name a few? Why did only four gospels end up in the canon while other such writings were excluded?

In the first place, as I have pointed out, the four gospels that now stand in the New Testament canon are without parallel in their antiquity. All four canonical gospels are normally assigned a date within the first century (although sometimes John, wrongly in my view, is dated as late as AD 110). No gospel outside of these four even comes close to being this early. The *Gospel of Judas* is decidedly Gnostic and written in response to Eucharistic church practices; it belongs to the mid second century. The *Gospel of Thomas*, I have argued at length elsewhere, should be dated to the end of the second century.[4] The *Gospel of Philip* belongs to the third century. Notice that none of these gospels approach the first-century dating of the canonical gospels. There are other gospels I could also mention, but the rule remains the same: any gospel outside of our canonical gospels is at least one generation later than our famed four (all of which were written within a few decades of one other), but in most cases the distance is at least a century. Anybody attempting to put these other gospels on the same historical playing field with the now-canonical gospels is simply playing fast and loose with chronology. The fourfold gospel collection remained impervious to latecomers because the four in question were considerably earlier; they were in a league by themselves.

The Gnostics could not dispute the priority of the canonical gospels, but they could and did dispute the claim that their gospels were any less apostolic. According to the Gnostics, Jesus taught a special truth to a select few. The teachings were passed along orally and in secret. Finally, the time was right to set the record straight about what Jesus said and, voilá, a *Gospel of Judas*, a *Gospel of Thomas*, a *Gospel of Philip*, among the rest. Apparently, the fact that the four gospels predated these Gnostic gospels by a considerable amount of time did not deter the would-be Gnostics from taking these texts seriously. But it should deter anyone who takes history seriously. There is something inherently suspect about the words of Jesus just showing up out of nowhere so long after the time of Jesus' death.

Another reason these noncanonical gospels failed to gain a hearing in the Great Church has to do with their theological content. Apparently, Ehrman would disagree. He seems to be saying that there was no canon, and no fourfold gospel canon within a canon, because there was no agreed-upon theology until much past the second century. But this simply isn't true. The *basic* continuity of Christian belief is clearly apparent when we consider, for example, how believers thought about Christ's humanity. When 1 John is written toward the end of the first century, its writer warns against those who disavow Christ's human nature: "By this you know the Spirit of God: Every spirit that confesses that Jesus Christ has come in the flesh is of God" (1 John 4:2). A few decades later, when Ignatius of Antioch writes to the Trallians, he tells them to "stop [their] ears" whenever they should meet someone who denies Jesus' humanity.[5] Roughly forty years after that, Justin accuses the same crowd of "robbing the flesh of the promise."[6] By the time we come to Irenaeus, writing toward the end of the second century, we find him saying, "And in every Epistle the apostle plainly testifies, that through the flesh of our Lord, and through His blood, we have been saved."[7] Around the same time, at the other end of the

Mediterranean world, Serapion, the bishop of Rhossus (Syria), is warning Christians under his jurisdiction against using the *Gospel of Peter*. The *Gospel of Peter* is problematic, he says, because it implies a nonhuman Christ.[8]

Despite Ehrman's assertion, this chorus of voices does not sound like a situation of "no agreed-upon theology." On the contrary, we can trace a hundred-year-old line, stretching from John to Serapion, and the message never changes: Christ came in the flesh, was crucified and raised in the flesh, and saves in the flesh. Those who did not share this theology were subverting the message of the gospel. On this point just about every church father seems to agree. While this may be only one example of an agreed-upon theology, one example is all we need to prove the point. If the second-century church distinguished at all between right belief and false belief, then we also would expect the same church to distinguish between those writings that reflected right belief and those that did not; that is, we would expect such a church to have a canon of sorts.

Clearly, there was an unflinching insistence on right belief when it came to the makeup of Jesus' body. Therefore, in asking us to imagine that the church operated without a corresponding notion of canon, Ehrman is in effect asking us to imagine the unimaginable. While there is no point at which the ancient church established a universal rule as to which gospels were "in" and which were "out," the church apparently didn't see the need for any formal pronouncement until the Reformation![9] It seems that the church didn't need a formal list of authoritative gospels any more than a mother would need an official list of her children. Guided by certain christological and historical convictions, the church hardly gave a moment's thought to any account of Jesus outside of the canonical four.

At the same time, we cannot definitively rule out the possibility that some of these later gospels may preserve some words of Jesus, independent of the canonical gospels. But in my judgment, if these noncanonical gospels do tell us something new about Jesus' words, such quotations are precious few and we have no way of corroborating them. Because the noncanonical gospels are so late and are largely derivative of the canonical gospels, the burden of proof rests on anyone hoping to claim that the former actually attest to the voice of Jesus.

It is striking that the four canonical gospels all depict Jesus in very human terms, quite unlike the way the Gnostic gospels present Jesus.[10] The church fathers I have cited above all take the same line: for them, Jesus must be human or he is nothing at all. It is primarily on account of this issue that the Christians (the proto-orthodox) distanced themselves from the Gnostics and refused to fellowship with them. But isn't all this narrow-minded? Why all the fuss about something as minor as whether Jesus was flesh or something else?

On a theological level, there are a number of ways to answer this question. I will limit myself to one: in denying Jesus' full humanity, the Gnostics were essentially denying that Jesus saved us as physical beings. If Jesus did not save us as physical beings but only, say, saved our spirits or souls, then that means he is not interested in saving the cosmos. In this case, too, humanity's relationship with the world is at best irrelevant. We are, then, as Jim Morrison sings, "riders on the storm." This is *not* our Father's world. The God who saves is *not* the Creator God. In that case, all things physical (our bodies, the things we do with our bodies, the things of history) don't matter. In fact, when you think about it, *nothing* matters except what goes on in one's spirit. We are essentially back to Buddhism.

The biblical vision is much broader and deeper than what Gnosticism had to offer. Jesus taught that his kingdom, the ultimate kingdom, would return creation to its proper created essence. Thus, when Jesus came bringing sight to the blind, enabling the lame to walk, and causing the deaf to hear, he was not simply doing a string of good turns. He was showing that his kingdom meant the restoration of creation, the world as originally ordered by God, before sin made a mess of things. He was beginning to reverse the chaos on a cosmic scale by putting into place a new creation. To understand anything less of Jesus is to misunderstand Jesus. Irenaeus and the second-century church knew what they were doing: the Gnostics had taken Jesus and ripped the teeth out of what he stood for, but they weren't about to get away with it, not at least without a fight.

But it was actually not the Gnostics who had to fight to stay alive; it was the Christians. And it was not the Christians who were sitting in the second-century equivalent of smoke-filled rooms, cutting deals as to what constituted right belief and what should be in the canon. The real powerbrokers of that world were the Romans. And the one thing the Romans wanted was allegiance to Caesar, that is, the Roman state. Because the Christians taught such revolutionary things as a new way, a new king, a new kingdom, and, to top it all off, the resurrection of the body, the Christians began to look pretty scary to the Romans. And so because the proto-orthodox believers would not swear by Caesar and because they would not deny the resurrection, the Romans took to persecuting them: this meant imprisonment, torture, and death. This is exactly the situation Irenaeus finds himself in when he writes that there must be four and only four gospels. Anyone who thinks the bishop of Lyons wrote these words as a bid for power doesn't realize that, as Irenaeus was well aware, it was actually a desperate call to preserve Jesus' mission from extinction at the hands of the Romans on the one side and the Gnostics on the other.

The Romans did not take to persecuting the Gnostics, because the Gnostics were, by contrast, much more flexible. "Caesar is lord? Fine!" "No bodily resurrection? Well, of course!" The Gnostics wanted to have Jesus, but at the very point at which identifying with Jesus' mission became politically or socially awkward, the Gnostics had a way of transmuting Jesus into their own ideal of a starry-eyed mystic or Greek philosopher. The Gnostics were not necessarily what you would call politically empowered (although the movement seems to have originated among an intellectually elitist class), but when push came to shove, they sided with those who were in power.

For present-day people who want to keep their Jesus but who also want to remain on the world's inside track, the seduction of Gnosticism can be overwhelming. If Jesus came to bring a religious, political, social, and economic revolution, then by siding with Jesus, you will inevitably find yourself in the uncomfortable position of siding against those who are now calling the shots. If Jesus came to say that the origin of evil lies in us, as humanity, this rubs against the grain of modern Western civilization, which is invested in the notion that humanity contains its own solution to its own problems. Following Jesus cannot be done by half measures; it is not for the faint of heart.

That summer, as I continued to read my Bible and observed the Jews for Jesus on Wall Street, I realized that the real power-brokers were not the ones cutting billion-dollar stock deals; nor were they the ones who made laws and policies; nor were they the ones who used violence to oppose such laws and policies. The real powerbrokers were those who refused to be cowed by what state and society deemed acceptable; instead, they attached themselves to an all-encompassing and deeply disruptive mission. Real power is the steady refusal to live out the script of the kingdom of the world. It is to live for a different kingdom, which is already being realized in the here and now.

ELEVEN
TRANSLATION WARS

If the full meaning of the words of scripture can be grasped only by studying them in Greek (and Hebrew), doesn't this mean that most Christians, who don't read ancient languages, will never have complete access to what God wants them to know? And doesn't this make the doctrine of inspiration a doctrine only for the scholarly elite, who have the intellectual skills and leisure to learn the languages and study the texts by reading them in the original? What good does it do to say that the words are inspired by God if most people have absolutely no access to these words, but only to more or less clumsy renderings of these words into a language, such as English, that has nothing to do with the original words?

—BART EHRMAN, *Misquoting Jesus*

I had seen abundance on the table, but I wasn't seeing it anymore. The family had finished eating. Dinner was now over and it was time to clear away the dishes. The boys were asking for dessert, so I said, "Sure, you can have dessert. But before we serve it, you first have to tell me what pi is."

"But we don't want pie—we want ice cream," one said.

"But I'm not going to give you any ice cream until you tell me what pi is," I insisted. Since I had just read in my son's weekly science newsletter that March 14 is National Pi Day, I decided—much to everyone's exasperation, I'm sure—to keep going with the pun to see if anyone would catch on to the fact that I wasn't talking about food but about a number.

Finally, one of the boys caught on. "Oh, *pi*! You mean 3.14."[1]

I did mean just that, and ice cream was served.

Of course, I *could* have responded differently. I could have been a stickler and said, "No, that's not quite right, Son. You see, 3.14 is merely an *approximation* for pi (π). You're going to have to do a little better than that."

On hearing that, my son, if he was particularly well studied, *might* have turned around and said, "Okay, 3.14159. Is that better?"

And on hearing that, I *might* have said, "No, not quite. Try again."

"Okay, 3.141592653589793. There. Can I have my dessert now?"

And if I really wanted to be an absolutely awful father in this hypothetical conversation, I could have said, "Listen, Son, we have calculated pi to beyond the millionth decimal place. I hear there's a fellow in Japan who has it memorized to seventy thousand places. Surely you can give me pi to, oh, say, the fifty thousandth place. I think that would be accurate enough for a nice big bowl of ice cream. Now let's have it."

Had I said that (and to be clear, I didn't), my poor boys would have wished that National Pi Day was never invented. They also might have concluded that their father was a very unusual and difficult man indeed. When schoolchildren are asked to solve problems with pi, it is usually not important for their purposes to go to the fifty thousandth decimal place. For most problems, 3.14 will do.

One of the interesting and little-known facts about pi is that it has its own holiday: National Pi Day, celebrated on March 14. On this day math teachers and other eager bodies get together, say a few kinds words in commemoration of this useful number, and eat—you guessed it—some pie. It is an informal national day, not an international event. This is because it is only the American dating format that has the month then the day of the month. In America 3/14 means March 14, but in most parts of the world, 3/14 would be nonsensical as it would indicate the third day of the fourteenth month. It is only when we translate pi into the American way of representing dates that we come up with March

14. There is a correspondence between pi and March 14, but this correspondence only makes sense to those who read and think in American English.

The absence of a fourteenth month in other systems has not deterred pi lovers outside of America from making do. Many in Europe celebrate Pi Day on July 22, because 22/7 (the twenty-second day of the seventh month) is a decent approximation of pi. It is another way of describing this reality of pi, and one that doesn't work for Americans (simply because for us Americans 22/7 means the seventh day of the twenty-second month and there is no twenty-second month). Meanwhile, in China they approximate pi by a different fraction, 355/113 (= 3.1415929). But in this case they celebrate not Pi Day but Pi Minute: the 355th day of the year (usually December 20) at 1:13 a.m. (= 355/113).

Now it goes without saying that if you celebrate Pi Minute, you're going to be far more accurate in your honoring of 355/113 (= 3.1415929) than all the riffraff who are content to celebrate Pi Day on March 14 (= 3.14). But then again, if you were an American who was not prepared to be one-upped by the Chinese, you could celebrate Pi Second on March 14 at 1:59:26 p.m., corresponding to 3.1415926. And if you wanted a *really* short celebration (one millisecond to be exact), you could set your watch for 3.1415926536. Obviously, this is hardly enough time for you to help yourself to a slice of key lime or Boston cream; nor is it enough time to say, "Happy Pi Millisecond." Even the fastest readers among us will be opening and reading our Happy Pi Millisecond cards either too early or too late.

There are, I suppose, two morals to this story. First, there are realities in the universe, including pi, that different cultures translate into their own worlds differently. The fact that Americans pencil in Pi Day on their March calendars while the British fit it into their July schedules and the Chinese observe it several days before Christmas does not mean pi is unreal or has no ability to tell you a circle's area (given the radius). The fact that we have different ways of mapping reality into our social and linguistic world does not invalidate reality, but only confirms that we as diverse, human creatures are born to translate. The second moral is this: accuracy is a fine thing, but it also can be overrated. In the case of pi, it surely would be tragic to allow an unrealizable ideal of accuracy to ruin not only a beautiful and generally comprehensible idea, but also a good party.

Looking back at my first two years at Johns Hopkins University, I now see that these two points are the very things I *didn't* understand as I was continuing my journey through the Bible. It was my freshman year and I had hooked up with a campus Christian organization called the Navigators. At that time, there was a guy named Dean who met me and took me under his wing. Having graduated from Hopkins, Dean was on his way to medical school. But he was first taking some time off from school to meet with people like me who showed an interest in learning more about God.

I was still working out what I really believed about Christianity. Since my senior year at Exeter, I had been continuing in my practice of *zazen*. But I never gave up on reading the Bible. Many mornings I would get up early, do a half hour of Buddhist meditation, then read the Bible. On the one hand, retrospectively, this might not seem like such a bad idea. A lot of Christians including myself could stand to slow down a bit and take the time to meditate rather than falling prey to the cultural myth of "I am productive; therefore,

I must be important." On the other hand, Buddhist meditation, because it is inescapably Buddhist in its assumptions, is a practice that is inconsistent with Christian belief. My feeling on these things purely came down to experience; in my thinking I was gloriously inconsistent. But then again, spiritual transitions often involve a growing realization of internal inconsistencies.

Dean was willing to work with me—Christian Buddhism and all. We developed a great friendship, which continues to this day some twenty-three years later. I became guilty of being an accomplice in Dean's conversion to Bob Dylan's music, something for which his wife, Cheryl, is still trying to forgive me. He was instrumental in my understanding the nature of what Jesus really said. Even more important, he was pivotal in making clear what Jesus' words meant for me.

You would think that after three years of reading the Bible, in Greek no less, I would know what Christianity was all about. Far from it. Because I had never seen examples of living faith, I had no context. It is the very rare Christian, indeed, who comes to faith through mere words on a page. Usually behind, in front of, and beside those words is a life. The life of an individual or a community—or both. And that life is the light of all humanity. This is almost necessarily the case because Christianity is not something that can be owned on a purely intellectual basis (as if it were an abstract set of ideas). Instead, Christianity must also be experienced from flesh to flesh through the Holy Spirit. After all, it is the Spirit, the Bible tells us, who is active among the Christian community and among those who find themselves convicted in regard to sin, righteousness, and judgment (John 16:8–10). Without an experience of the Holy Spirit, you will never own Christianity for yourself. More exactly, you will never be owned by the kingdom of God. When God's hand is poised to lay claim to one of his children, that hand can almost always be discerned within the ragged glove of human life.

Under Dean's tutelage I began memorizing verses from the English Bible. The translation Dean used was the New International Version (NIV). So, as a gift, Dean bought me something called the Topical Memory System. This Topical Memory System basically consisted of sixty flash cards with sixty different verses drawn from the NIV. Soon not only was I reading Scripture, but I was also meditating on it and memorizing it—even before I really understood what it meant.

By the fall of my sophomore year of college, Dean had gone off to New Jersey for medical school and I had compiled a long compendium of verses that I had memorized from the NIV. By that time, too, I was meeting with other Christians who also were memorizing Scripture. On a weekly basis we would meet, read the Bible together, and test each other on our memory work. When we did this, we agreed right off the bat that the recital of our memory work had to be exactly word for word—after all, this was God's Word, and you wouldn't want to mess it up.

One evening while my friends and I were testing ourselves, and I was either being stumped or stumping someone else on the exact wording of the memory verse, it occurred to me that the NIV was *just* a translation. Now, of course, I knew as well as anyone that the New Testament was first laid down in Greek. But in the process of keeping yourself and others to an exact word-for-word rehearsal of the translation, you can be lulled into the impression that the biblical writers wrote not in Greek but in English—the English of the NIV. And so why did we insist on word-for-word accuracy anyway? For a time there seemed to be a disconnect between the fact that the New Testament was first written in Greek and the fact that we had, in a compulsive sort of way, to get the wording of the NIV just right.

Of course the NIV, first published in 1978, was not the first English translation, nor has it been the last.[2] The first English Bible was composed in 1382 on the basis of the Latin Vulgate by John Purvey and Nicholas of Hereford, two students of John Wycliffe. A second, slightly more dynamic version appeared six years later. Unfortunately, it met with stiff opposition. In 1415 the so-called Wycliffe Bible was condemned and burned; in 1428 Pope Martin V ordered that Wycliffe's rotted corpse be exhumed, burned, and scattered on the river. Despite its rough reception, the Wycliffe Bible became very popular and would have an impact on later translations.

Using the Hebrew and Greek texts, William Tyndale published his English Bible in 1526. Tyndale's act was considered so heinous that he was kidnapped, smuggled out of Antwerp, and made to face trial leading to his execution. Before he was strangled to death, Tyndale's last words are reputed to have been "Lord, open the king of England's eyes." Like the great humanist Erasmus, Tyndale desired to base his new translation not on the Vulgate of the church but on versions written in the language of the original texts.

Other English Bibles followed, including the Coverdale Bible, Matthew's Bible, the "Great Bible," the famed Geneva Bible, and the Rheims-Douay Bible. But the greatest English Bible of all was to be the King James Version of 1611, also called the Authorized Version. King James VI of Scotland was interested in a new Bible, to be sure, for certain political and ecclesiastical reasons. But there seems to be indication that he had a more personal interest in the project as well. Taking an active role in administering the project, he hired some of the best readers of Hebrew and Greek in England (some of whom had begun their language study at age five or six). James wanted an English Bible that would end all English Bibles. For a long time, he got his wish. It wasn't until the late eighteenth century that anyone dared challenge the beauty and clarity of the King James Bible.

In the twentieth century, we have seen more than a fair share of Bibles come off the press: the American Standard Version (1901), the Revised Standard Version (1952), the Jerusalem Bible (1966), the New English Bible (1970), the New King James Version (1982), and the New Revised Standard Version (1990), to name only a few. All said and done, in the past hundred years there have been more than three dozen translations of the New Testament into English. While countless people groups have no Bible in their own language, we English readers luxuriate in a vast assortment.

But sometimes the multiplication of Bible versions feels more like a burden than a luxury. The wide range of Bible translations, which becomes obvious in almost any setting where ten or more Christians bring their personal Bibles, has created its own kind of crisis of confidence: Why are there so many different Bible translations? How do we know which ones to trust? More to the point of this book, if the various English translations put Jesus' words in different ways, how can we know that the words of Jesus haven't been lost?

But you don't have to be an English speaker, inundated with

various possibilities of translation, to realize that there is no "one and only" translation out there. In the first four centuries of the Christian church, there was an exorbitant number of Latin translations, some good, some bad. Some were based on the Greek text, while others were based on earlier Latin texts. There were other versions as well. As the gospel spread to parts of the world outside of Palestine and the missionary paths of Paul, it also became necessary to translate the Bible into a number of tongues, including Syriac, Coptic, Gothic, and Ethiopic. It is interesting to note that for many of these ancient versions, the first translations were rather dynamic, giving the sense of the Greek text in a rather free way. But as time went on and later generations sought to know the Scriptures more precisely, their translations became more precise. Surges of nationalism no doubt also had an influence on creating, say, a Syriac translation that made for a very suitable next-best-thing-to-the-Greek.

Had I known back in college about all these translations, modern and ancient, I would have felt all the more confirmed in my point. Since my English Bible is merely a translation of something approaching the original texts, and since there are many other translations out there that often have different words, doesn't this whole business of translation seem arbitrary? Doesn't it make all this talk of "God's Word" dishonest?

At the time, I was becoming convinced that this was the case. At the time, too, it became something of a convenient point given my spiritual state. In those years I was learning a lot about the Bible and about what God was asking of me through Jesus Christ. But you can't keep taking in this knowledge without somehow responding to it: either by obeying or by blunting it. In a disturbing way, because

I could read the Bible in Greek and my Christian friends could not, I was able to use that knowledge as a way of neutralizing—at least in my mind—the results of *their* biblical interpretation. "Sure, this is what you think," I would say inwardly, "but if you *really* knew what the Greek says, you would know that it's not as cut-and-dried as you think." And if my Christian acquaintances oversimplified their interpretation of Scripture because they did not know the Greek, surely they also must have been oversimplifying the way they looked at Jesus Christ, salvation, and all this business about following him. Having some expertise in one limited aspect of biblical interpretation, I often inwardly looked down my long nose on those naïve folk who supposed that we could be so sure of what the Bible really said. Once you've established your superiority to other readers of Scripture in your own mind, it's a short step to feeling that you're superior to the Bible and, in a sense, God himself. Proud people make for bad listeners in regard both to people and to God.

Insider knowledge is, in fact, a very common strategy for putting off God and his claims on us. Most of us, at one time or another in our lives, will resort to the same strategy of one-upmanship practiced by the child on the playground who tauntingly chants, "I know something you don't know. I know something you don't know." When you know something other people don't know, you feel powerful. It's like holding the last trump card when all the other trump cards have been played.

No one is immune from the temptations associated with the perception of having knowledge. Some people use knowledge to acquire power. Consider, for example, the pompous pastor who remarks in his sermon, "Now, people, if you're going to understand this passage at all, you absolutely need to understand that this

English word 'chaos' in your simple translations actually comes from the Greek word *chaos*, meaning, er, 'chaos.'" Some preachers use their seminary training to illuminate the text and strengthen the people. But others, sadly, use knowledge as a way of saying, in a socially acceptable way, "I know something you don't know."

Others use knowledge as a means of maintaining power, even power over God. "You say that Jesus was raised from the dead? But I know something you don't know: people don't rise from the dead." "You say that Jesus is the only way? But I know something you don't know: Jesus went to the East to learn from the Buddhists." "You say that this is what Jesus says. But I know something you don't know: the Greek actually says something entirely different, and besides, his actual words have been lost in transmission." Whether the knowledge be accurate, fallacious, or completely unexamined, we all have, at least once in our lives, used the pretension of knowledge to keep God at bay. A little knowledge can be a dangerous thing.

And yet despite my pose of moral and intellectual superiority, I could not completely dismiss these Christians. They had something I did not have. They had a wellspring of joy and a peace that I was only taking in by small sips. They pretty well knew what they were about in life. They knew who they were and weren't put off by people who challenged them in their faith.

Unfortunately, I could not say the same for myself. I was still sorting myself out. I was on the fence and finding it a difficult place to sit. On the one hand I was spending more time with Christians, but on the other hand I was feeling an increasing pull to be a "normal person" who did "normal things," which of course serious Christians would not consider doing. My life was becoming increasingly fragmented, split apart by my inconsistencies. I would go to church just because my Christian friends went to church, but more often than not I would go hung over from a hard bout of Saturday night drinking. At the time I did not feel it was in my best interest to broadcast this fact at church, but perhaps ultimately it would have been. Confession, another word for honesty, can be a helpful thing.

But honesty was not the path I was about to tread. All along I tried my best to make sure that one crowd (the church crowd) knew as little as possible about the other crowd (the fraternity crowd). All the while I had studiously kept my two worlds, my two lives, apart. Not that it was a matter of my having to choose between two sets of friends. (After all, Jesus is famous for having gladly spent most of his time with the nonreligious types.) The question was more fundamental: whose values would I adopt? Or, put another way, whose kingdom would I live for?

In an odd way, the fact that there were many supposedly legitimate Bible translations that were at remove from the original Scriptures was one of the many things that helped me stave off the force of God's Word. People could quote the NIV to me; I could quote it to myself. But in order to deflect what it was saying, I could always tell myself, "This isn't God's Word; it's only a *translation* of God's Word. The vast majority of the church does not have God's Word. And if the church doesn't have God's Word, then how seriously should we take this Jesus kingdom thing anyway?"

I didn't know it at the time, but my thinking was very flawed. It was based on all the wrong assumptions, assumptions I inherited from the Enlightenment. I was assuming that Christians, in order to be Christians, had to know the contents of their Bibles in a precise way. And if they couldn't know their Bibles in a precise way, then they couldn't very well do God's will or enjoy his divine desserts. But this is silly. It would be like a father telling his son that he has not *really* learned pi until he has learned it to the fifty thousandth decimal place. The schoolchild who learns pi does so with as much accuracy as is necessary, no more and no less than what you need to solve the next problem. Should the same schoolchild go on for a PhD in mathematics, more nuance and more accuracy would presumably be in order because the problems would require it. But until such a time, it would be absurd to deny that 3.14 is pi simply because there are more precise ways of denoting pi. No matter how many digits you use to represent pi, whether three or three hundred thousand, your representation will only be an approximation—more precise than some approximations but not as precise as it could be.

Bible translation works in much the same way. For most readers of the English Bible, the English they read is adequate for their purposes. Should the same readers seek more precision in terms of word-for-word equivalences, these are available, but there is a price to pay for such translations. They are usually less readable. So we have a decision to make. Do we go for readability or semantic precision? It's not an easy decision. If the more readable yet less precise Bible is more understandable, then there is a sense in which the less precise Bible is, in fact, more accurately conveying the Word of God!

In approximating the Greek of the Bible, as with approximating pi, sometimes less precision is warranted if it helps yield a clearer understanding. We should remember that just as it is not the mathematician's goal to know pi for its own sake, so we, too, are not called to study Scripture for its own sake. If pi was derived in order to ascertain the area of a circle, then the Scriptures were derived from God in order that we might know this God and make firm our salvation by obedience. God is far more interested in our responding to the knowledge of his revelation than in our refining it. Sometimes we just have to draw the circle, even with an imperfect knowledge of our pi.

This point should put our anxieties about translation into perspective. While the student of Scripture who knows the lexical meaning of the original languages certainly has an advantage over the reader who knows only English, it is only a relative advantage. No matter how well you know Greek (and no modern-day reader compares with the long-gone ancient speakers), there are countless realities in and behind the biblical text that you can only just begin to fathom. The relativity of our knowledge does not void our reading of Scripture or make it irrelevant. We might all have varying degrees of precision in representing our pi, and different cultures might represent the number in different ways, but this does not make our pi any less real. The words of Jesus have come to the church in translation, but does this absolve us from responding—and celebrating?

CONCLUSION
BREAK ON THROUGH
TO THE OTHER SIDE

I kept reverting to my basic question: how does it help us to say that the Bible is the inerrant word of God if in fact we don't have the words that God inerrantly inspired, but only the words copied by the scribes—sometimes correctly but sometimes (many times!) incorrectly?

—BART EHRMAN, *Misquoting Jesus*

It was just after dawn on a cold November Saturday morning in 1983. I had been up all night drinking beer and talking with my friend Greg, who lived just outside of the Baltimore beltway. I was due to get back to my fraternity house near the Hopkins campus because someone was picking me up first thing in the morning so that we might go to a Navigator conference in Annapolis, Maryland. I wasn't entirely sure what the conference was about or why I even signed up for it in the first place. But I was told that if I went, I just might have my "socks blessed off." So I agreed to go and was not about to back out. *Maybe*, I inwardly thought, *I really will be blessed.* As it turned out, for me this was to be no mere Navigator conference; it was an appointment with God.

I got back to my place with some time to spare, so I proceeded to take a shower and put on some music. I was still listening to the Doors in those days. One of my favorite Doors songs had a driving beat that made you want to get up and dance, or roll around on the ground, or do something frantic with your body. The song was called "Break On Through to the Other Side."

What the "other side" was for Jim Morrison, I will never know.

Unconsciousness? Subconsciousness? Another dimension of the universe accessible only through drug-induced stupor? I don't know. But I believe that Jim Morrison and John Lennon were saying two very different things.

Morrison's life, it seemed to me, was a desperate, but ultimately frustrated, attempt to get to some other side. He didn't know what the other side was, or how to get there, but there was something inside of him that told him that here-and-now visible realities were but the surface of a much larger reality.

Lennon, on the other hand, asked us to imagine that there was nothing "below us" and "above us, only sky."[1] Once we do that and once we forget about divisively robust and transcendental hopes, Lennon seems to be saying, we will be freed up to live for today. More than that, we will become a brotherhood of man. Morrison says, "Break on through to the other side"; for Lennon there is no other side. This is it.

There is one more line to Lennon's ditty. He says that to imagine all this is "easy if you try." And he is right. It is easy to imagine a world where what you see is what you get—no more, no less. It's easy to imagine because the world's Western culture has been living it for the past few hundred years. I have known some people who grew up in the projects and didn't know any better until they got out. While the Enlightenment project has brought us some positive things, its greatest tragedy is that we have grown up in it without knowing anything different, without knowing a God who speaks into our reality. And just as the projects of the 1960s are one example of an establishment's loftiest dream becoming someone else's greatest nightmare, so, too, our culture has been forced to enjoy the horrible freedom that the Enlightenment has demanded.

The postmodernist philosopher Jean-Françoise Lyotard gets it right when he looks back on modernity's attempt to offer an all-encompassing story that explains reality and declares the attempt a failure. Coming to terms with the moral, spiritual, and aesthetic shallowness of the Enlightenment, a shallowness that "Imagine" shares, the age of postmodernity is now attempting to explain reality in an ever-increasing variety of ways. Distrustful of the "this is the way it is" dogmatism of the Enlightenment, the post-modern age has turned to its own proliferating number of narra-tives, its own stories as to where we have come from and where we are going. But postmodernity, like modernity, has not been able to escape the tyranny of its own individualism. As Lyotard laments, "Each individual is referred to himself. And each of us know that our self does not amount to much."[2]

Not that I was thinking about any of these things as I was get-ting cleaned up before the conference. I was just trying to sober up and feel like a human being again. Before I knew it, my ride had arrived. It was time for the music to be over, to turn out the lights and break on through to the other side. Little did I know that in the days and months and years to come, I would feel more human than ever.

The main speaker for this day-long conference was an elderly gentleman by the name of Bob Boardman. When I sat down with a big cup of coffee in hand to hear his talk, I immediately realized he was speaking though a voicebox. At first this was very distract-ing. But as he began to explain why he spoke through a voicebox, the deep and gravelly words issuing from the podium only under-scored the content of his message.

It seems that he had been captured by the Japanese in World

War II. During his detainment he was treated very badly. At one point, a Japanese soldier without provocation took a bayonet and rammed it into Bob's throat. Bob lived but lost his vocal cords. When the war was over and he found himself still alive, rather than returning to the States, Bob decided to stay in Japan and become a missionary to the nation of his captors. He stayed in Japan for decades, telling people about the love of Jesus Christ. "Pray," he told us, "that people might turn from Buddhism to Jesus Christ."

But wait a minute, I thought, he can't say that. I *am* a Buddhist. A Buddhist *and* a Christian. For a moment I was offended. But then as I sat there and listened and struggled, I realized that as much as I wanted Christ and Buddha, Boardman was right. You can't sit before Buddha and follow one who says, "I am the way and the truth and the life." You have to decide on your kingdom. You have to decide whether Jesus is the King he claimed to be. And if you choose not to decide, that itself is a decision—a decision against Jesus Christ.

When it was time for another coffee break, I decided against yet another infusion of caffeine and chose instead to take a walk. I needed some time to think and get myself sorted, once and for all. I decided that I would keep walking in a straight line down the street until I had made a decision on which side of the fence I belonged. The world I had known—the world of Lennon and Nietzsche—would have been quite compatible with Buddhism. But the world that was breaking in on and all around me—that was not. I kept walking and thinking, praying and walking, walking and thinking. I was doing a lot of walking, but I was getting nowhere.

Yet suddenly, for some inexplicable reason, I stopped in my tracks. I stopped not because I had it all figured out. Nor did I stop because it was extremely cold (although it was). I stopped because I knew it was time to turn around. Some people turn around gradually as they grow into a knowledge of God. Other people's turning around is like an event. I had been growing into a knowledge of God for about four years, but that was the day, that was the moment, I believe, that I turned around. Not everyone has a moment like this. But I did.

The Bible has a word for this turning around: repentance. Repentance doesn't come when we've figured it all out. It doesn't come once we've gone to graduate school and decided that Jesus' words were not lost in transmission after all. It doesn't come after reading a book about the words of Jesus. Repentance comes when God shows us that it is not God or Jesus' words that have been lost in transmission, but it is we ourselves who have been lost in transmission.

The other side of the coin of repentance is faith. When the Roman centurion stood before the cross, heard Jesus' cry of dereliction, and saw how he died, he declared, "Truly this Man was the Son of God!" (Mark 15:39). The passage is as intriguing as it is mysterious. Why would this (presumably) pagan stranger to Jesus have concluded that Jesus was the Son of God? And why did he come to this conclusion (in Mark's mind, the right conclusion) while the confused and frightened disciples had all fled the scene with their hearts heavy with despair?

The answer, I think, is in the text of Mark itself. He saw *how* Jesus had died. Well, how did Jesus die? We have glimpses here and there through the four gospels that get at how he died, but no one verse, no one gospel, makes clear just how he died. I think the point is this: in determining that Jesus was the Son of God, the centurion did not proceed by a single fact or syllogism, as if being the Son of God could be proved. Rather, he proceeded by a kind of divinely inspired aesthetic reasoning. I think there was for the centurion, as there was for me in November 1983, a divinely initiated convergence of beauty. As I tell my students, when you think of crucifixion, you are thinking of one of the most horrific ways for a human being to die. But as becomes clear in the Gospels, when you read how Jesus died, you see he died just as he lived. He died a beautiful death. The centurion needed no text critic, no historian, to tell him who Jesus was. He just knew: Jesus was the Son of God. When this objective reality breaks into our subjective experience, it changes everything. It pulls us into a new kingdom.

Does this mean history doesn't matter for the centurion or for those of us who have come to agree with him on Jesus? Certainly not. History matters very much. But we must realize the limits of history. To begin with, as Ehrman himself rightly points out, the facts of history don't tell us anything. Facts are silent things—until they are interpreted. Once we begin to interpret, however, we are weaving those facts into the tapestry of our political commitments, suspicions, trusts, loves, desires, memories, impressions, and, above all, imaginations.

Ehrman imagines a reconstruction in which the words of Jesus, while making their long journey from the first century until now, have been subject to all kinds of revision. Such revision comes in the first instance from the earliest community, then from the gospel writers, then from the scribes, then from the translators. The extent of the revision has been massive. For all intents and purposes, Jesus' words have been lost in transmission. To be sure, Ehrman's account is not inherently implausible.

But "not inherently implausible" is not the same thing as probable. In this book I have offered a counter-reconstruction, one that I believe is more probable. I believe that Jesus' words, precisely because they were revered as authoritative from the beginning, were seized on by the gospel authors and reduced into writing with the greatest care. Later copyists who transmitted these gospels in turn had such unsurpassable regard for the gospel writers that they took great pains to faithfully preserve these gospels and, within these gospels, Jesus' words. The words of Jesus that we have today in our modern-day English translations are equivalents and approximations, but they are indeed the words of Jesus.

To be clear, this does not mean that our English texts are word-for-word identical with what Jesus actually said. Clearly, they are not. Jesus' words were modified as they were translated from Aramaic into Greek. The gospel writers would often take the thrust of Jesus' words and put it in their own words. This is the nature of translation and storytelling. In years following, the scribes would pass along these words, making mistakes along the way, yes, but also constantly correcting and constantly seeking to preserve the words of Jesus as best they could. Judging by the very high degree of agreement among our manuscripts, even if that transmission was less than completely perfect, it was faithful. Finally, modern translators have taken up the best reconstruction of the original Greek text and have sought to approximate the sense as best they can for the audience they seek to reach. These translations are the inspired Word of God because they are historically rooted in the inspired words as they were contained in the very first gospel texts.

Ehrman's recounting of how the words of Jesus have been lost in transmission reminds me of another story. It's the familiar story of the hero who, through applying methods and reasoning, is able to unmask the prejudices and superstitions of parochial folk who have never properly taken the time to explore the matter properly and scientifically, or even to think for themselves. Once, however, such superstitions are debunked, once it is again demonstrated that there is no "other side" to break through to, society will be free indeed. Free to do what we want to do. It's an old and tired Enlightenment script, underpinning countless other narratives, ranging from the French Revolution to just about every episode—for those old enough to remember the show—of *Scooby-Doo*.

But I have another script that draws its principles not from the Enlightenment but from a theological understanding of God's Word. This is not so much my script as the way in which the church has traditionally understood things. You might say it is a scriptural understanding of history. It goes like this: Jesus Christ came into the world as the embodiment of God. As God, his nature was unchangeable, for God does not change. But as man, he grew in wisdom and in stature (Luke 2:52). The revealed Son of God is both eternal and dynamic. As it is with Jesus Christ the Word of God, so it is with God's Word contained in Scripture. It is eternal and will never pass away (Mark 13:31), but there is a dynamic element as well. As we in the church continue to pass along God's Word, preserving it and interpreting it, we continue to grow in our understanding. We are not alone in this process. God sends his promised Holy Spirit to guide us. Down through the ages God superintends the transmission of his own Word and works among those in the church who have been authorized as Scripture's interpreters. Even as we have very good historical grounds for believing that we have Jesus' words preserved in transmission, there are also theological grounds as to why this might be: God was not sovereignly at work only in the Christ-event. Through the Spirit, God also has been active in the interpretive recording of that event and the transmission of that record down to this day. The Spirit also guides the church in its interpretation of that record: the Spirit is active in, through, and despite the plurality of ways in which Scripture is understood and applied.

Some might see this story as being unfair to history, as if it were a priori not permitted for God to intervene in history. But any objection against this understanding of transmission simply does not see that in ruling out divine superintendence, one has already ruled out the possibility of objective revelation. Because God has revealed himself decisively and objectively in Jesus Christ, it is impossible—at least if we are to take it on its own terms—to understand the Bible any differently than this. God's Word requires no stamp of approval from the ancient historian or text critic. Instead, it requires our assent. Our heeding God's Word is not frustrated by the historical distances over which Scripture has been carried; our heeding God's Word is frustrated by our wills, which are instinctively set on a kingdom that opposes God.

When modern-day scholars wax eloquent on the problematic history of Jesus' words, an unstated assumption about the nature of the evidence and knowledge is usually lurking in the background. When Ehrman describes his own break from Christian fundamentalism in order to adopt an agnostic position, I wonder if this move is actually as radical as he makes it out to be. On the level of religious affiliation, the move is huge. But on the level of epistemology, the question as to how we come to a knowledge of God, he apparently hasn't budged much. When Ehrman as a young man and a young Christian came to believe the Bible to be God's Word, he acted on the basis of certain empirical truths. This becomes evident from the fact that his finding an alleged error in Jesus' naming Abiathar as high priest brought down his whole doctrine of the Word. Once one element of uncertainty entered into the mix of things, *everything* suddenly became uncertain—and therefore, in short order, unverifiable and thus untrue.

The notion that we believe the Bible to be God's Word on certain proofs is not a biblical notion; it is a notion of fundamentalism inherited from the scientific age. The one who thinks that the Bible can be *proved* as God's Word will undoubtedly be disappointed. There are difficulties in the Bible; there are things that simply cannot be easily harmonized in the limited scope of our reasoning. So if you come to believe the Bible is the Word of God on the basis of your ability to verify its absolute coherence, once you are no longer able to verify that coherence, once you find data that admit no handy explanation, your belief suddenly becomes destabilized. By playing the Enlightenment's rule of nothing is true unless it's verifiably true, nothing is certain unless it is absolutely certain, a number of Christians have failed to realize that they are walking very near to the bear trap of utter skepticism.

The revealed Word of God, precisely because it is a personal revelation from a personal God, can be neither proved nor disproved as divine. Its inspiration does not follow from anything we have to say about it. It is objectively inspired because it is from God. Our subjective impressions and inquiries regarding Scripture may leave us with certain tensions, but they cannot be the basis on which we determine the Word of God. We must begin with a basic decision regarding the kingdom of God. One of the myths of historical inquiry is that we can have an honest conversation about Scripture as a historical object entirely apart from our assumptions about this kingdom. In my view, the integrity of Jesus' words speaks for itself, and those who support and deny this view do so by firing their imagination on somebody's torch. Needless to say, not all torchbearers serve the same kingdom.

When in July 1969 Neil Armstrong stepped out of the lunar module onto the moon's surface, people around the world heard him say, "One small step for man, one giant leap for mankind." Most people seem to have agreed that the famous astronaut flubbed his one and only scripted line. Armstrong's repeated insistence that he did say, "One small step for *a* man . . ." seems to have fallen on deaf ears.[3]

Recently, however, a computer analysis of the initial transmission has yielded the conclusion that Armstrong, in fact, did say just that: "One small step for a man." The precise wording of the original utterance was lost in transmission due to static. On the one hand, this changes very little, for with or without the "a," it is clear what he meant. On the other hand, it is a point that should be noted: having established our best reconstruction of the transmission, we see that the astronaut stands vindicated.

This is not entirely unlike the way it is with Jesus' words. There has been some degree of static between Jesus' mouth and the modern ear. This cannot be denied. Nonetheless, our inability to get every last word down with utmost certainty hardly invalidates his message. Jesus' voice is preserved in transmission. Besides, the more historians look into this voice and its material reverberations through history, the more we find a basic integrity to the transmission we have. All this only anticipates a fuller, clearer revelation to come.

Whatever you believe about Jesus, or come to believe about Jesus, the written recollection of his words is not something that can be lightly dismissed. No amount of wishing or imagining can change this fact. The question now is what to do. When Jesus, who broke into our world from the other side, came teaching and preaching, he came in order that we might be free. Free to surrender, free to live, and free to hope—all within a kingdom that will never perish, spoil, or be lost in transmission. Has Jesus really spoken of such a kingdom in our hearing? Imagine if he has.

ACKNOWLEDGMENTS

My thanks go to the folks at Thomas Nelson—Greg Daniel, Matt Baugher, and Thom Chittom—as well as to my friends who have commented on the manuscript with more general thoughts and reflections (Mary Mehaffey and Woody Dunstan). Thanks go also to Chris Spano for his footwork on the footnotes and a *fortiori* to David "Go-Uncle" Vinson, who devoted himself not only to a close reading of the manuscript but also to me. Most of all, I wish to thank my wife and soul mate, Camie. She remains my biggest encouragement.

NOTES

Introduction

1. Mark Noll, *The Scandal of the Evangelical Mind* (Grand Rapids: Eerdmans, 1994).

2. Bart Ehrman, *Misquoting Jesus: The Story Behind Who Changed the Bible and Why* (New York: HarperSanFancisco, 2005), 9.

Chapter 2

1. John Dominic Crossan, *The Historical Jesus: The Life of a Mediterranean Peasant* (New York: HarperSanFranciso, 1992), 395–416.

2. See for example E. M. Blaiklock, *Jesus Christ: Man or Myth?* (Nashville: Thomas Nelson, 1984).

3. For example, the richly allusive use of *logos* ("word") in the first chapter of John invokes, among other things, the Stoic doctrine of the rational mind sustaining the universe; mention in Titus 3:5 of our renewal (*palingensia*) surely points back to well-established Greek mystery language.

4. At times, the arguments of parallel-therefore-influence are almost silly. For example, plate 2 of their book shows three pictures: the first of a third-century BC Egyptian statue of a queen nursing a child on her lap; the second, a Roman painting of a first-century BC woman nursing a child on her lap; the third, a thirteenth-century AD Byzantine icon of Mary holding (and not nursing) Jesus on her lap. The caption reads: "Christian representation of the Madonna and baby Jesus were based on ancient Pagan images of the miraculous child Osiris-Dionysus and his divine mother." Perhaps it did not occur to the authors that when the late-medieval artist rendered the infant Jesus on his mother's lap, he could have been inspired by something more immediate than a statue from another part of the world that preceded him by well over a thousand years. After all, down through the ages, mothers have been known now and then to hold their babies on their laps.

5. Erik Hornung, *Conceptions of God in Ancient Egypt: The One and the Many* (Ithaca: Cornell University Press, 1982), 138.

6. See my "On Raising Osiris in 1 Corinthians 15," *Tyndale Bulletin* 58 (2007), 117–28.

7. For the classic and definitive argument, see A. J. M. Wedderburn, *Baptism and Resurrection: Studies in Pauline Theology Against Its Graeco-Roman Background* (WUNT 44; Tübingen: Mohr Siebeck, 1987).

8. Eusebius, *Ecclesiastical History*, 3.39.3–4.

Chapter 3

1. Friedrich Nietzsche, *Human, All Too Human: A Book for Free Spirits*, vol. 3 of *The Complete Works of Friedrich Nietzsche*, trans. R. J. Hollingdale (Cambridge: Cambridge University Press, 1986), 19–20.

Chapter 4

1. Now, as I understand, revised and retitled as *The World's Religions: Our Great Wisdom Traditions* (New York: HarperSanFrancisco, 1991).

2. Gotthold Lessing, *Nathan the Wise*, act 3, scene 6.

3. As far as I know, it is only Marcus Borg who attempts this in, for example, his very popular *Meeting Jesus Again for the First Time* (New York: HarperCollins, 1994). But by insisting on Jesus' Jewishness and combining this with a vision of personal existentialism and social egalitarianism, Borg is, I think, merely attempting to have his cake and eat it too.

Chapter 5

1. C. K. Barret, N. T. Wright, E. P. Sanders, etc.

2. This is recognized later in the New Testament writings outside of the Gospels, e.g., Eph. 2:20; Rev. 21:14.

Chapter 6

1. Rudolf Bultmann, *The History of the Synoptic Tradition* (New York: Harper & Row, 1963 [1921]); Martin Dibelius *From Tradition to Gospel* (ET New York: Charles Scribner's Sons, n.d. [1919]); Karl Schmidt, *Der Rahmen der Geschichte Jesu: Literarkritische Untersuchungen zur ältesten* [Jesus: Literary-Critical Investigations into the Oldest Jesus Traditions](Berlin: Trowitzsch and Son, 1919).

2. This is true even when the sources of evidence are seen as very reliable. For example, even if we could get Jesus on videotape, that doesn't prove anything. Just like anything else, videotape recordings also can be doctored. Seemingly, "spontaneous" recordings also can be the result of skillful production. Doubt attends every historical certainty, to a greater or lesser degree, making history itself disputable.

3. The only exceptions to this rule would be where Jesus speaks in Aramaic (e.g., Mark 5:41; 15:34).

Chapter 8

1. Irenaeus, *Against Heresies*, 3.11.8.

2. Ehrman, *Misquoting Jesus*, 35.

3. The Doors, "Riders on the Storm" *L.A. Woman*, Rhino CD, 2007.

Chapter 9

1. It is possible that there were in fact more than twenty-seven "books" to begin with. For example, some scholars have seen the fourth gospel as a composite of different sources (autographs); others see our text of 2 Corinthians as being made up of several Pauline letters.

2. See Ehrman, *Misquoting Jesus*, 17–20.

3. This is demonstrated, for example, by the astonishing degree of similarity between what used to be our oldest complete Hebrew Bible, Codex Leningradensis (datable to AD 1008), and the Qumran texts (250 BC–AD 50).

4. Ehrman, *Misquoting Jesus*, 50–51.

5. Ibid., 216.

6. Ibid., 215.

7. Ehrman argues this out more fully in *The Orthodox Corruption of Scripture: The Effects of Early Christological Controversies on the Text of the New Testament* (New York: Oxford University Press, 1993).

8. This was the Gnostic Heracleon, who was active the first quarter of the second century.

9. Irenaeus, *Against Heresies*, 2.28.1.

10. David C. Parker, *The Living Text of the Gospels* (Cambridge: Cambridge University Press, 1997), 4.

11. There are other considerations here as well, e.g., the strength and antiquity of the so-called Western text, which diverges from what is widely considered the picture of the perfect lawn: the Alexandrian text.

12. Homer's *Iliad* is the closest runner-up, boasting almost seven hundred extant manuscripts. From there the number of manuscripts available for any given classical text drops off dramatically.

13. By my count in Mark 1:1–16:8 there are 3,992 words attributed to Jesus, and only 28 of these (.7 percent) are subject to any serious question. But these involve questions such as the presence or absence of the article "the," whether a given command was issued in the present or perfect ("Stand up!" versus "Having stood up!"), or whether a given noun takes a certain grammatical ending (which effects no change in meaning).

Chapter 10

1. See Ehrman's *Lost Christianities: The Battle for Scripture and the Faiths We Never Knew* (Oxford: Oxford University Press, 2003) and *Lost Scriptures: Books That Did Not Make It into the New Testament* (Oxford: Oxford University Press, 2003).

2. See the discussion on this passage in chapter 8.

3. See James A. Kelhoeffer, *Miracle and Mission: The Authentication of Missionaries and Their Message in the Longer Ending of Mark* (WUNT 2.112; Tübingen: Mohr Siebeck, 2000), and Theo K. Heckel, *Vom Evangelium des Markus zum viergestaltigen Evangelium* (WUNT 2.120; Tübingen: Mohr Siebeck, 1999).

4. The dating of this gospel is highly debated. For a recent defense of a late-second-century dating, see my *Thomas, the Other Gospel* (London: SPCK; Louisville, KY: Westminster John Knox, 2007).

5. Ignatius, *Epistle to the Trallians*, 9.1–2.

6. Hermann Samuel Reimarus, *Fragments 2*.

7. Irenaeus, *Against Heresies*, 5.14.3

8. Eusebius, *Ecclesiastical History*, 6.12.2–6.

9. Even Athanasius's famous festal letter of AD 367 does not attain to the status of being a universally binding document. It is only in the Reformation and Counter-Reformation of the sixteenth and seventeenth centuries that Protestants and Roman Catholics took official pains to enumerate the books of the New Testament.

10. It is on this point that Dan Brown's character Lea Teabing has the matter absolutely backward. See *The Da Vinci Code* (New York: Doubleday, 2003), 234.

Chapter 11

1. Pi (π) is the number used to determine the area of a circle (pi times the radius of the circle squared).

2. For more on this discussion, see the excellent survey in Bruce M. Metzger's *The Bible in Translation: Ancient and English Versions* (Grand Rapids: Baker, 2001).

Conclusion

1. John Lennon, "Imagine," *Imagine*, Capitol CD, 1971.

2. Jean-Françoise Lyotard, *The Postmodern Condition: A Report on Knowledge* (Minneapolis: University of Minnesota Press, 1984), 15.

3. In his book *Chariots for Apollo: The Untold Story Behind the Race to the Moon* (New York: Avon, 1985), Charles R. Pellegrino and Joshua Stoff cite Armstrong as follows: "There must be an 'a.' . . . I rehearsed it that way. I meant it that way. And I'm sure I said it that way."

LaVergne, TN USA
29 January 2010
171574LV00002B/1/P